NATIONAL COUNCIL FOR THE SOCIAL STUDIES

POWERFUL

STANDARDS-BASED

ACTIVITIES

NCSS

EDITED BY WILLIAM W. WILEN

National Council for the Social Studies
3501 Newark Street, NW
Washington, DC 20016
www.socialstudies.org

TODAY'S SOCIAL STUDIES
Creating Effective Citizens

Library of Congress Catalog Card Number: 00-109513

Copyright © 2000 National Council for the Social Studies. All rights reserved.
Printed in the United States of America.

ISBN 0-87986-084-7

First printing, October 2000

10 9 8 7 6 5 4 3 2 1

Table of Contents

Roman numerals indicate the thematic strands of the NCSS Curriculum Standards for Social Studies to which the lesson plans are most relevant.

The Social Studies Standards Movement and Powerful Teaching: From Congress to the Classroom 5
William W. Wilen

Images of the West 13
Peggy Altoff and Sari Bennett
I **II** **III** *Middle School/High School*

Trade Routes in the Old Northwest — 1790-1850 23
Cameron Buckland
II **III** **VII** *Eleventh Grade*

Surveying Japanese Students: Comparing Students from Different Cultures 31
William P. Fitzhugh
I **IV** *Grades 3-5*

The Culture of Native Americans 37
Larry Fontanarosa
I *Eighth Grade*

Constantine Village Cemetery — A Bridge to Today 43
Elvin W. Keith III
II *Eleventh Grade*

Unions and Collective Bargaining 47
Mike Koren
VII *Sixth Grade*

Transportation on the Move 53
Paula Ann Mulford
I **II** **III** *First Grade*

Glidden's Patent Application for Barbed Wire 57
Emily Ray and Wynell Schamel
II **VII** *Middle School/High School*

Two Tickets to Freedom 63
Patricia King Robeson
III **VII** *Fifth Grade*

Prejudice and Values 71
Walter F. Urbanek
Ⅱ Ⅴ Ⅵ *Ninth Grade*

Simulation on Ethical and Moral Citizen Responsibilities 77
Helen O. Willey
Ⅵ Ⅹ *High School*

Uncovering Pompeii: Examining Evidence 81
Michael M. Yell
Ⅱ *Middle School*

Global Reflections in Economic Decision Making 91
Suzanne C. Zaremba
Ⅶ Ⅸ *Third Grade*

The Ten Thematic Strands of the
NCSS Curriculum Standards for Social Studies

Ⅰ **CULTURE**

Ⅱ **TIME, CONTINUITY, AND CHANGE**

Ⅲ **PEOPLE, PLACES, AND ENVIRONMENT**

Ⅳ **INDIVIDUAL DEVELOPMENT AND IDENTITY**

Ⅴ **INDIVIDUALS, GROUPS, AND INSTITUTIONS**

Ⅵ **POWER, AUTHORITY, AND GOVERNANCE**

Ⅶ **PRODUCTION, DISTRIBUTION, AND CONSUMPTION**

Ⅷ **SCIENCE, TECHNOLOGY, AND SOCIETY**

Ⅸ **GLOBAL CONNECTIONS**

Ⅹ **CIVIC IDEALS AND PRACTICES**

The Social Studies Standards Movement and Powerful Teaching: From Congress to the Classroom

William W. Wilen, Kent State University, Kent, Ohio

The 1990s may well be characterized as the era of the standards movement as educators look back ten to twenty years from now. From that vantage point, they will have the answer to a question that we would all like to have now—have the results of this massive effort to reform the outcomes of education been successful or not? Educators can't wait for hindsight, though; they need to make curricular decisions based on what they read, think, and know now. One intention of this NCSS publication is to help social studies teachers who are preparing students for active citizenship, and teacher educators who are preparing the teachers of these students, to implement the various national and state standards in their classrooms. The other, and primary, intention is to illustrate how this classroom implementation can be achieved through the application of the powerful teaching and learning principles devised by National Council for the Social Studies (NCSS).

How did we get to this point of winding down a whirlwind decade of debating, planning, articulating, and disseminating national standards? Where are we in implementing them? Where do the state standards fit in this process? What is the role of the powerful teaching principles? Most important, how can teachers be assisted in accommodating this new curricular and instructional direction in their classrooms? First, how did we get to this point?

The Standards Movement

Goals 2000, a term that brings either an optimistic smile or sarcastic frown, but rarely a neutral expression, was the rallying cry of the governors at their national conference in 1989. Five years later legislators in Congress mouthed this buzz word as they approved the goals and started a pipeline of funding to states that submitted improvement plans. The eight idealistic goals providing the direction for the effort were designed to address public concern about the low levels of student academic performance and the poor showing of students' performance in international assessments. Included in the eight goals was one on developing competency in the content areas of civics, economics, history, and geography. Critics argued that not all the social sciences were represented and, also, that social studies, as a discipline of integrated social sciences, was not represented.

With the advent of national education goals, the need arose to have voluntary national standards in the content areas. Congress responded with funding for content-specific professional organizations to identify key content and outcomes in their subject fields. The National Council for Teachers of Mathematics had led the way with the publication of its standards in 1989, which reflected its vision of the direction that mathematics education should take. The National Center for History in the Schools produced the first standards for K-12 world and U.S. history courses only to have them roundly criticized by primarily conservative groups, and eventually they were rejected in Congress. Although they were revised in 1995, they still are controversial. The Center for Civic Education, the Geographic Education Standards Project, and the National Council on Economic Education followed with their own sets of standards reflecting visions of the direction their respective disciplines should take.

NCSS Curriculum Guidelines

In the early 1990s National Council for the Social Studies set up a task force of members to develop a broad framework for organizing the social studies curriculum. It was intended that this effort would produce our nationally recognized standards. Working without federal funding, NCSS approved and published *Expectations of Excellence: Curriculum Standards for Social Studies* in 1994. They are significantly different from the individual social science standards in that the ten K-12 themes are derived from key interrelated concepts from the seven social sciences, and the themes are interdisciplinary. The reason for the different perspective lies in the civic competence purpose of social studies, which is much broader than content-oriented goals: "To help young people develop the ability to make informed and reasoned decisions for the public good . . .".[1] NCSS expected the social science content disciplines to support the purpose of the social studies standards because they provide content depth ensuring an important component of a quality program. As such, the NCSS Standards can "serve as a framework or umbrella under which the other social studies disciplines can find a home."[2] Other major differences from the social science standards are that the NCSS Standards pay major attention to how students can be taught the conceptual themes and how their progress might be assessed. These naturally become key concerns when thoughts are given to putting the standards into operation for practical application in the classroom.

What are the NCSS Standards? In many ways, the NCSS Standards ". . . offer a vision of what might be, an image of what is possible."[3] Alleman and Brophy have identified a variety of operating assumptions:

■ The standards emphasize the development of civic competence through interdisciplinary social education, which is based on major understandings drawn from the social sciences and supportive disciplines;

■ The standards reflect the values of NCSS in that they are only a guide to states and school districts, not to be imposed or demanded;

■ The standards do not guarantee that limited student exposure to the key ideas will increase understanding and appreciation;

■ The standards assume that the states and districts will assume responsibility for specifying the content supporting the strands, including content enhancements that go beyond the basic standards, and the selection of content resources;

■ The standards document includes example lesson scenarios that are based on the principles of powerful teaching, which are suggestive of how the standards might be implemented in K-12 classrooms;

■ The standards document calls for a systematic and rigorous assessment adapted to local district's needs but compatible with the national standards.[4]

Will the NCSS Standards succeed? It's too early to tell, but there are strong indications that the standards are being incorporated into state curricula as the states update and revise their curricula. Among the many reasons for their appeal is that they are broad and encompassing whereas the social science discipline standards are focused. In his review of the national history standards, Saxe projected that the NCSS Standards may become very appealing to teachers and curriculum specialists because they are more reasonable, comprehensive, flexible and "doable," but also because the NCSS Standards have not been reviewed as controversial.[5]

Powerful Teaching Principles

What is the role of powerful teaching? A major strength and another difference between the NCSS Standards and content standards is the emphasis placed on how the interdisciplinary themes might be taught in the classroom. Curricular documents rarely address instructional considerations of the content to be taught at any level of comprehensiveness and depth. It is usually left up to the district's curriculum supervisor and teachers to devise ways to implement curriculum instructionally. NCSS has been very innovative and insightful in dealing with classroom implementation of the new curriculum by publishing its "Vision of Powerful Teaching and Learning in the Social Studies: Building Social Understanding and Civic Efficacy." It was first published as a separate document in 1992 and then included as a supplement to the curriculum standards. The principles of powerful teaching are a vision of how the civic competence purpose of social studies might be instructionally achieved in the classroom. While the interdisciplinary themes give teachers the "what" that should be taught, the powerful teaching principles suggest "how" it should be taught.

The principles of powerful teaching and learning have been synthesized from research studies and represent key features of ideal social studies instruction. They "represent an emerging consensus of expert opinion about how to teach social studies for understanding, appreciation, and life application."[6] Many educators consider the powerful teaching principles the current state of the art and science of social studies teaching and learning.

Social studies teaching and learning are powerful when they are meaningful, integrative, value-based, challenging, and active. These five principles are briefly summarized:

■ **Meaningful**—social studies content is meaningful when it relates to achieving the social understanding and civic efficacy goals of social studies. Students learn networks of knowledge, skills, beliefs, and attitudes that connect to life inside and outside school. Content is taught in-depth to promote understanding, appreciation, and life application.

■ **Integrative**—social studies is integrative in its treatment of topics and issues across the social sciences and broader curriculum. It is integrative across time and space, and it is integrative of technology. It is also integrative of knowledge, skills, beliefs, values, and attitudes with action inside and outside the classroom and community.

■ **Value-based**—social studies is committed to democratic principles and social responsibility. The ethical dimensions of topics are considered, and controversial issues are addressed. Students' value-based and well-supported positions, particularly in relation to the process of decision making, are encouraged.

■ **Challenging**—social studies emphasizes the development of inquiring minds within an atmosphere of reflective thought and discussion. Collaboration and cooperative learning activities are encouraged.

■ **Active**—social studies emphasizes the active construction of meaning through reflective thinking and decision making. An application of "learnings" is achieved through interactive discourse and other authentic teaching and learning activities.[7]

One of the major purposes of the standards is to "provide examples of classroom practice to guide teachers in designing instruction to help students meet performance expectations."[8] Indeed, the standards document provides numerous scenarios of how the standards might be generally applied in teachers' classrooms. There are two or three scenarios illustrating each of the themes for the early grades, middle grades, and high school. The value of these scenarios is that teachers can immediately get an impression of the themes in action. The scenarios illustrate how the powerful teaching and learning principles can be specifically used in daily lesson planning by teachers at all levels. One of the drawbacks is that they are somewhat artificial in that they portray interested and engaged students being taught by teachers with unlimited curricular resources and instructional expertise.[9] Although the scenarios provide a snapshot of what might be, they do not contain the specific information necessary for successful implementation in the real world classroom. Detailed lesson plans that demonstrate the application of the curricular themes and principles of powerful teaching that are created by teachers based on their classroom experiences would be of more value to teachers.

State Curricula and Standards

Two years ago, the NCSS Instruction Committee solicited lesson plans from NCSS members through *The Social Studies Professional* that represented exemplars of powerful teaching. Of those received, eleven met the criteria and were prepared for publication. The lesson plans represent the efforts of teachers in two eastern states (Maryland and Virginia) and three midwestern states (Michigan, Ohio, and Wisconsin). To determine how closely the teachers' plans conformed to their state social studies standards and how closely the state standards matched up with the NCSS Standards, the five sets of standards were secured and analyzed.[10]

All five states had revised their curricula at the time the NCSS Standards came out in 1994 or have revised them since then. The Michigan, Ohio, and Wisconsin state standards are very closely associated with the NCSS Standards, especially in terms of the purpose of social studies and the specific themes/strands identified. The Maryland and Virginia standards evolved more around the traditional subject areas.

Further analysis showed that each lesson plan matched up to its respective state's thematic strands and/or achieved the specified learning goals. In terms of the NCSS Standards, each plan matched up to a minimum of one thematic strand, and maximum of three strands, and achieved a minimum of two, and maximum of eleven, performance expectations. None of the state documents included the NCSS powerful teaching and learning constructs, and none offered any instructional suggestions as to how the standards might be achieved. We can conclude from this limited sample that the NCSS Standards document is having a curricular impact on some state documents, particularly in terms of social studies purpose and content organizers, but that it is not having an instructional influence related to how teachers might implement methods and strategies to meet the standards. Assuming that the curricular influence of the NCSS Standards continues to grow in its impact on state documents, the principles of powerful teaching should become more relevant and essential because this is what teachers want and need to accomplish their instructional role. The proverbial "bottom line" for teachers when faced with implementing major curricular changes is how can these standards be realistically put into practice in the classroom?

The Lesson Plans

The lesson plans included here are comprehensive and detailed. They are what teachers need to test their hunches about the practicality of the application of the standards in their classrooms. Our intent is to bring alive the interaction of the standards' themes, performance expectations, and principles of powerful teaching. We attempt to accomplish this through the presentation of teacher-produced and classroom-tested lesson plans. As such, they reflect exemplary thinking and doing in a variety of K-12 social studies classrooms and subject areas. They are offered "in the hope that classroom teachers will create social studies experiences for students that take the field to a new level of power and meaningfulness."[11]

Thirteen lesson plans were selected for this project, eleven directly solicited from teachers and two additional ones identified from current NCSS publications.[12] The two additional ones were selected because their inclusion allowed the project to illustrate the teaching of all ten NCSS themes. The thirteen represent all three of the major levels: early grades (three), middle grades (five), and high school (five). All ten of the NCSS thematic strands are represented at most of the levels with ❶ TIME, CONTINUITY, AND CHANGE, and ❼ PRODUCTION, DISTRIBUTION, AND CONSUMPTION being dominant. The emphasis of the history-oriented strand is fairly characteristic of traditional K-12 education in the United States while the economics-oriented strand is reflective of a growing trend.

Most of the thirteen lesson plans identify the relevant NCSS thematic strands, describe their powerful teaching features, clarify a purpose/rationale, list objectives and resources, specify a time allotment, detail a procedure, and describe the assessment. In addition, most of the plans include extension activities and appendixes of attached materials and handouts to put the lesson into practice. Some of the plans include alternative assessment approaches. The plans are summarized below:

1. Peggy Altoff and Sari Bennett focus on the West in the first lesson because of its fascination and misconception for most middle school U. S. history students. Through cooperative learning groups, thoughtful discussion, and the use of primary sources, students compare and analyze their own and others' perceptions of the West.

2. Cameron Buckland uses interdisciplinary social science inquiry to stimulate students to discover historical generalizations that have application to their world of today. His eleventh grade U.S. history students have to solve a problem of determining which route and what methods of transportation during the early 1800s would have enabled traders to maximize their profits.

3. William P. Fitzhugh encourages his elementary students, through a questionnaire, to examine aspects of their personal identity and compare them with Japanese students who responded to the same survey. Students analyze the results of both questionnaires and depict the data in graph form. This then serves as the basis for discussion examining cultural similarities and differences.

4. Larry Fontanarosa knows that his middle school level U. S. history students have preconceived ideas about Native American peoples. Using a variety of group learning activities that involve the aural and visual senses, and discussion, he encourages them to reflect on the plight of Native Americans in the past to make connections to today.

5. Elvin Keith takes his high school U. S. history students to their community cemetery to help them to understand the past and how it relates to the present. Students "do" history as they engage in an in-depth exploration of a person selected from a cemetery headstone using a wide range of school and community resources.

6. Mike Koren's sixth graders explore the actions of unions, particularly collective bargaining. As a capstone activity, he engages his students in a simulation about the process of negotiating the contract of a hypothetical company during which they have to consider many viewpoints and the impact of their decisions.

7. Paula Mulford uses students' keen interest in transportation to compare different forms and their changes from past to present. First grade students apply their "learnings" as they construct timelines and transportation models.

8. Emily Ray and Wynell Schamel have students learn about the invention of barbed wire to illustrate how this nineteenth century technological achievement affected different groups of people associated with the settling of the West, through several wars to peacetime today. Guided discussion and group work are used to involve high school U.S. history students in examining Joseph Glidden's invention and considering how ordinary classroom objects might be improved.

9. Patricia King Robeson uses a powerful story of a slave couple that escapes to freedom to stimulate her fifth graders to analyze the issue of slavery. Students engage in a variety of interdisciplinary learning activities that involve cooperative learning groups, ethically based discussions, chart construction, and slave song verse creation.

10. Walter Urbanek knows that all students have prejudices. In his lesson for ninth grade global studies students, he first has students examine their own attitudes and beliefs related to discrimination and prejudice. They then explore instances of genocide in preparation for an investigation of a national group that has undergone extreme prejudice.

11. Helen Willey uses the excitement of a simulation to teach eleventh grade government students the responsibilities of citizens in a democracy. Students plan, enact, and evaluate an antiabortion demonstration, and this is used as a springboard into a debate of the ethical and moral obligations of citizens who demonstrate to change public policy.

12. Michael Yell begins the inquiry lesson with a puzzling event that his middle school world culture students need to solve. Using cooperative learning groups, he has his students engage in an in-depth study of a past civilization from historical, geologic, and archaeological perspectives.

13. Suzanne Zaremba realizes that economics has little meaning for her third graders because parents usually hand out the money for the necessities. The purpose of her lesson is to involve them in the inquiry process to teach basic economic concepts and global connections. They accomplish this in cooperative learning groups as they build Japanese houses.

Conclusion

Our intent with this project was to demonstrate to teachers how specific NCSS thematic strands, performance expectations, and powerful teaching principles can be realistically integrated and applied in social studies classrooms through comprehensive and exemplary lesson plans. Although not all grade levels, subject areas, and performance expectations are represented in the thirteen plans, there is sufficient information for teachers to make useful and practical connections to their own teaching situations. The scenarios contained in the NCSS Standards document are very helpful as an initial impression in encouraging teachers to consider the possibility of applying the standards. But the specific lesson plans included here, hopefully, will inspire teachers to say, "This could work in my classroom!" 📰

Endnotes

1. National Council for the Social Studies, *Expectations of Excellence: Curriculum Standards for Social Studies* (Washington, D.C.: National Council for the Social Studies, 1994), 3.
2. Michael Hartoonian and Margaret Laughlin, "Social Studies Standards: A Pathway to Professional Development," *Social Studies and the Young Learner* 8, no. 1 (1995): 30-32.
3. S. G. Grant, "Nightmares and Possibilities," *Social Education* 59, no. 7 (1995): 443.
4. Janet Alleman and Jere Brophy, "NCSS Social Studies Standards and the Elementary Teacher," *Social Studies and the Young Learner* 8, no. 1 (1995): 4-8.
5. David W. Saxe, "The National History Standards: Time for Common Sense," *Social Education* 60, no. 1 (1996): 44-48.

6.   National Council for the Social Studies, *Expectations of Excellence*, 158.

7.   *Ibid.*, 162-170.

8.   *Ibid.*, 13.

9.   Grant, "Nightmares and Possibilities."

10. Maryland State Department of Education, *Maryland School Performance Assessment Program* (Baltimore: Maryland State Department of Education, 1992); Maryland State Department of Education, *High School Social Studies Core Learning Goals* (Baltimore: Maryland State Department of Education, 1997); Board of Education, Commonwealth of Virginia, *Standards of Learning* (Richmond: Board of Education, Commonwealth of Virginia, 1995); Michigan State Board of Education, *Social Studies Vision Statement and Content Standards and Benchmarks* (Lansing: Michigan State Board of Education, 1996); State Board of Education, *Social Studies: Ohio's Model Competency-Based Program* (Columbus, Ohio: State Board of Education, 1994); State of Wisconsin, Department of Public Instruction, *Wisconsin's Model Academic Standards for Social Studies* (Madison: State of Wisconsin, Department of Public Instruction, 1997), www.dpi.state.wi.us/standards/ssintro.html.

11. Alleman and Brophy, "NCSS Social Studies Standards and the Elementary Teacher," 4.

12. William J. Fitzhugh, "Surveying Japanese Students: Comparing Students from Different Cultures," in *Tora No Maki II: Lessons for Teaching about Contemporary Japan* (Washington, D.C., and Bloomington, IN: National Council for the Social Studies and ERIC Clearinghouse for Social Studies/Social Science Education, 1997), 35-39; Emily Ray and Wynell Schamel, "Glidden's Patent Application for Barbed Wire," *Social Education* 61, No. 1 (1997): 53-56.

Appreciation is extended to the NCSS Instruction Committee for its assistance in making this publication possible. In particular, Jere Brophy's help in initially soliciting the lesson plan manuscripts was essential in getting the project in motion. Cameron Buckland's help in initially analyzing the state curriculum guides and standards also needs to be appreciatively acknowledged.

Images of the West

Peggy Altoff, Carroll County Public Schools, Westminster, Maryland, and
Sari Bennett, University of Maryland, Baltimore County, Maryland

Grade Level/Subject: Middle School and High School—U. S. History

NCSS Thematic Strands:

❶ CULTURE

d. explain why individuals and groups respond differently to their physical and social environment and/or changes to them on the basis of shared assumptions, values, and beliefs (Middle Grades); and

b. predict how data and experiences may be interpreted by people from diverse cultural perspectives and frames of reference (High School).

❷ TIME, CONTINUITY, AND CHANGE (High School)

d. systematically employ processes of critical historical inquiry to reconstruct and reinterpret the past, such as using a variety of sources and checking their credibility, validating and weighing evidence for claims, and searching for causality; and

e. investigate, interpret, and analyze multiple historical and contemporary viewpoints within and across cultures related to important events, recurring dilemmas, and persistent issues, while employing empathy, skepticism, and critical judgment.

❸ PEOPLE, PLACES, AND ENVIRONMENTS (High School)

g. describe and compare how people create places that reflect culture, human needs ... and current values and ideals ...

Key Features of Powerful Teaching and Learning

Meaningful—through thoughtful discussion, students examine their current images of the West, analyze the images of people a century ago, and compare the two;

Integrative—the content provides opportunities for students to read primary source material and listen to the words of author Wallace Stegner, and using knowledge and skills taught in other disciplines, students communicate orally, in writing, and through drawing;

Challenging—student thinking is challenged as students analyze primary resources that include varying perspectives and conflicting images of the West, and they are further challenged to participate assertively but respectively in discussions and cooperative learning activities; and

Active—students process content by relating it to what they already know (or think they know) about the West. In addition, authentic activities are emphasized as students use critical thinking to develop a class description of the West, then, through comparison with actual descriptions, find a reason to refine it.

Purpose/Rationale/Introduction

The West remains a region of fascination and misconception for most middle and high school students. Their images of its settlement, development, and expansion are formed more by popular media—television and movies—than by primary and/or secondary source material. This interactive lesson uses the cooperative learning "jigsaw" technique. After developing a class paragraph that captures their current collective image of the West, students work in "expert" groups to examine one of four images. Then, in teams consisting of one member from each expert group, they analyze all images. Finally, students match images with pictures the teacher has collected or draw a picture and reexamine the paragraph written by the class to determine its accuracy.

Objectives (Students will):

a. use prior knowledge and information from an audiotape to develop a written description of the West;

b. work in groups and teams to examine and analyze descriptions of the West written by individuals who participated in its development;

c. use knowledge from a variety of primary sources to analyze different cultural and social perspectives of the West;

d. select or draw visual images (pictures) that accurately reflect the written images examined and analyzed; and

e. complete a writing assignment evaluating the accuracy of "the real West" as reflected in written and visual images.

Time Allotment: one to two class periods

Resources Needed

1. audiotape of attached script or similar selection (optional; see appendix);

2. numbered pictures of the West, gathered by the teacher from various sources, placed on the bulletin board. These can be selected from calendars, textbooks, and pages marked, or bookmarked Internet sites;

3. four worksheet descriptions of the West labeled in different ways (see appendix); and

4. drawing materials.

Procedure

1. Motivation

Discuss the following: What is your image of the West? How would you describe it? Have students Think-Pair-Share a list of words or phrases they would use to describe the West. Jot responses on the chalkboard or on a transparency. Note: If students lack background knowledge required to brainstorm this list, select four quotes—one from each page. Write these on the chalkboard or on a transparency. Have students discuss the images suggested by these quotes.

(Optional: Read and/or listen to "Introduction" from the audiotape *A Sense of Place*. As students listen to the tape, ask them to jot down words or phrases that describe the West. Change or add to the original responses, expanding the descriptive list on the chalkboard or transparency.)

With the class, use the list to develop a short paragraph on the chalkboard, a transparency, or on poster or chart paper, summarizing student images of the West. Use a paragraph starter, such as "The West is a region of . . .". Display this paragraph where all students can see it.

2. Activities

Ask students the following: What would people who lived in the West during its development in the late nineteenth and early twentieth centuries think of our description? Would women agree or disagree? Why? African Americans? Children? Native Americans? How could we find out?

Distribute quotation sheets labeled in four different ways (see appendix). (Note: Quotes are in their original form. They have not been corrected for grammar and/or spelling.)

Have students with quotation sheets labeled the same way form groups. If these are too large, create two groups of students with the same labeled quotation sheets. Have students investigate the image of the West in the written description (quotes) found on their sheet; then discuss the following:

a. In what ways are the images of the West described by these people like the image we developed?

b. In what ways are the images of the West described by these people different from the one we developed?

Form teams of four students, with each student having a quotation sheet labeled in a different way. Have each student on the team summarize orally the image of the West as described in the quotes he/she read. As a team, have the four students decide:

a. Which image of the West was most like that developed by the class? Explain the reasons for the selection. (Have students refer to posted paragraph.)

b. Which image of the West was most unlike that developed by the class? Explain the reasons for the selection. (Have students refer to posted paragraph.)

(Optional: Have each team of students meet with one other team to discuss its decisions and the reasons for agreement or disagreement.)

Poll the class to determine decisions of the teams. Discuss reasons for agreement or disagreement among teams.

Assessment

Have each student select a partner with a quotation sheet labeled the same way. Have this pair review the image of the West in the quotes on its sheet, then write a summary of this image in a few sentences. Next, have each pair view the numbered pictures of the West displayed on the bulletin board or chalkboard, select the one that best matches the written description it has created, and provide reasons for its selection.

As time allows, these can be shared with other pairs or with the class as a whole.

(Note: If the teacher is unable to find pictures, have each pair of students draw a picture that reflects its written description. These can be posted to complete the rest of the assignment.)

Criteria for Evaluating the Assessment:

1. To what extent did the student work cooperatively with his/her partner?

2. To what extent did pairs write a summary of the image they examined?

3. To what extent did pairs select (draw) an appropriate picture?

4. To what extent did pairs provide reasons for their picture selection (drawing)?

Alternate Assessment
Writing Assignment—Provide students with the following:

Your class has been studying descriptions of the West. Some students say these descriptions, both written and pictured, provide an accurate image of the West, while others say they do not tell about or show the "real West." What do you think?

Write a paragraph defending your point of view on the question. Before you begin, you may want to think about the pictures you have seen, the descriptions (quotes) that you have read and shared, and the summary you have written.

Now write a paragraph defending your position on the question, Did the descriptions you examined, written and visual, provide an accurate image of the West?

Criteria for Evaluating Alternate Assessment
1. Did the student write a paragraph?

2. To what extent did the student state his/her position on the question clearly?

3. To what extent did the student use information from the written and visual images examined to defend his/her position?

Conclusion
Discuss how students' images of the West changed as a result of completing the activities in this lesson. Refer back to the paragraph written during the motivation and ask how they might change it.

Ask students if anything in the quotes from African Americans, Native Americans, children, or women surprised them. Ask if the investigation led to any new questions about the West that they would like to have answered.

Extension Activities
1. Find and examine images of the West created in the descriptions of immigrants to determine whether or not they support the images examined in this lesson.

2. Read descriptions of the West found in textbooks. Compare these to the images of children, African Americans, women, and Native Americans examined in this lesson.

3. Have students evaluate the sources used. Which do you think were the most accurate? The least accurate? Why?

Note: The term Indian peoples can be used interchangeably with Native Americans. 🔳

Transcription from Wallace Stegner, "Introduction," *A Sense of Place* [audiotape]
(Louisville, Colo.: Audio Press, Inc., 1989):

"I seem to have been born with an overweening sense of place, an almost pathological sensitivity to the colors, smells, light, and land and life forms of the segments of the earth on which I've lived. With another kind of childhood, I would probably have grown up as localized and territorial, as protective of my own small stamping ground, as a sage grouse. But my childhood was wandering, and instead of being able to root myself securely in one place, I had to adapt to a series of them. Migratoriness, while not especially good for my self-confidence, did make me a native—not of any particular town or state—but of the whole West. On the face of it, that sounds preposterous. The whole West extends from the 98th meridian to the Pacific, and from below the Rio Grande to above the 49th parallel.

It's not a region as the Midwest is a region, but a map full of sub-regions, covering parts of three nations. It contains the widest plains, the highest mountains, and the deepest and driest valleys on the continent. And it is combed by the wildest winds anywhere—tornadoes, blizzards, Chinooks, Santa Annas, and blue northers. Its people are as various as its topographies and weathers, a real melting pot mix of red, white, brown, yellow, and black. Its history is a composite of conquest and purchase, boom and bust, pipe dream and myth. And in the popular imagination—as in the horse operas on which the popular imagination feeds—history and time no longer exist in the West. Both stopped, it is said, in 1890, when the American frontier was declared closed. The Western past is timeless, the Western present discontinuous and, in effect, irrelevant.

How can you be native to anything so confused and contradictory as that? The answer is about like the answer of the cattleman who was asked how he managed to make a living when he lost $30.00 on every cow he raised. 'You do it on volume,' he said.

To become a native to a lot of places you live a lot of places. You move around a lot. And if you take pains to do your moving always west of the 98th meridian, in country that has always been too dry to develop in the ways of other regions, then you can't help becoming habituated.

Everything that the West means . . . space, emptiness, distance, clarity of air, sparseness of flora and sparseness or mobility of fauna . . . lots of public land and lots of federal bureaus to manage it . . . even the mindset of optimism for the big strike, the get-rich-quick dream that ends so often in defeat and disillusion . . . all that stems from the abiding fact of Western aridity, the same fact that dries your nostrils and cracks your lips. One look, one sniff of the wind, one glimpse of scruffy grass and pervasive earth colors—gray and tan and rusty red and tone white . . . one moment of realization that chlorophyll is not the color of this world . . . will tell me or any Westerner that he's at home. If that Westerner is like me, it will also tell him that he is where he wants to be, and that being where he wants to be involves him in problems as well as perceptions . . . angers as well as delights.

For the West has not been settled rationally. It has been raided over and over for one resource or another. And its economics have been the economics of liquidation. Eighty-five years ago, Mary Austin, in *The Land of Little Rain*, warned us, 'The manner of the country makes the usage of life there,' she said, 'and the land will not be lived in except in its own fashion. The Shoshones live like trees with great spaces between.'

Instead, we have dammed rivers and made gardens in rattlesnake and chuckwalla country. Eventually, the land will take them back. Meantime, for the native, there is this mixture of nostalgia, regret, anger, and love. Response to the West is no simpler than the West itself."

Appendix

Quotation Sheet #1: Women

They have just three seasons here, winter and July and August.[1]

If you do not drive me to a cleaner place to camp and sleep tonight I will take my blankets and go alone. . . . Our tents stand in what we should style a barnyard at home and I am sure if I were there I should as soon think of setting a table there as in such a place. The stench is sometimes almost unendurable, it arises from a ravene that is resorted to for special purposes by all the Emigration, but such things we must put up with.[2]

I would make a brave effort to be cheerful and patient until the camp work was done. Then starting out ahead of the team and my men folks, when I thought I had gone beyond hearing distance, I would throw myself down on the unfriendly desert and give way like a child to sobs and tears, wishing myself back home with my friends and chiding myself for consenting to take this wild goose chase.[3]

I did not like [it] very well but after we had taken our claim and became settled once more I began to like [it] much better. . . . the summer is beautiful and not hot a very little rain tho it is not so warm in the summer here as it is in the States the nights cool and comfortable and I can sleep like a rock. the winter is rather rainy, but it is not cold and so bad getting about as it is in the States here the grass is fresh and green the year round and our cattle are all fat enough now for beef their is not a month in the year but I can pick wildflowers or some strawberry blossoms.[4]

Trudging along within the sight of the Platte, whose waters were now almost useless to us on account of the Alkali, we one day found a post with a cross board pointing to a branch road which seemed better than the one we were on. . . . We decided to take it but before many miles suddenly found ourselves in a desolate, rough country that proved to be the edge of the "Bad Lands" I shudder yet at the thought of the ugliness and danger of the territory. Entirely destitute of vegetation the unsightly barren sandstone hills, often very high and close together formed of great bowlders piled one on top of the like glaciers, with ravines and gulches and between and mighty full of crowching, treacherous Indians. . . . [5]

Child's grave . . . small pox . . . child's grave . . . [We] passed 7 new made graves. One had 4 bodies in it . . . cholera. A man died this morning with the cholera in the company ahead of us . . . Another man died. . . . Passed 6 new graves. . . . We have passed 21 new-made graves . . . made 18 miles. . . . Passed 13 graves today. Passed 10 graves. . . .

June 26	Passed 8 graves
June 29	Passed 10 graves
June 30	Passed 10 graves . . . made 22 miles
July 1	Passed 8 graves . . . made 21 miles
July 2	One man of [our] company died. Passed 8 graves . . . made 16 miles [6]

It blew up a little cooler towards sunset and we travelled pretty well, to make water was our object, both man and beast were craving it. . . . Now, about dark, we came into the musquito regions, and I found to my great horror that I have been complaining all this time for nothing, yes absolutely for nothing; for some two or hundred or even thousands are nothing compared with what we now encountered . . . . Millions upon millions were swarming around me, and their knocking against the carriage reminded me of a hard rain. . . . [7]

We Hidatsa women were early risers in the planting season; it was my habit to be up before sunrise, while the air was cool, for we thought this the best time for garden work. Did young men work in the fields? (laughing heartily) Certainly not! The young men should be off hunting, or on a war party; and youths not yet young men should be out guarding the horses. Their duties were elsewhere, also they spent a great deal of time dressing up to be seen by the village maidens; they should not be working in the fields.[8]

Well I will try to tell you what my work is here in this muddy Place. All the kitchen that I have is four posts stuck down into the ground and covered over the top with factory cloth no floor but the ground. . . . This morning I awoke and it rained in torrents . . . I went and lookek into my kitchen. The mud and water was over my Shoes I could not go into the kitchen to do any work today but kept perfectly dry in the Dining. . . . I felt badly to think that I was detined to be in such a place. I wept for a while and then I commenced singing. . . . Three times a day I set my Table which is about thirty feet in length. . . . sometimes I am feeding my chickens and then again I am scareing the Hogs out of my kitchen and Driving the mules out of my dining room.[9]

. . . Here there are no class distinctions in society; all are on equality. Leave the land of oppression and come to free Kansas.[10]

I had on good clothes, a big overcoat and overshoes . . . but I couldn't keep warm no how to save my life. I was done cold all the time. Kansas is a good place but it didn't suit me at all. . . . It is prairie and the wind blows there pretty hard, and I don't know what to think of the country at all.[11]

School didn't start till the middle of the winter. They just had four months a year. Had two in the winter and two in the summer. They tried to have school when it wasn't the right time for the children to be working in the fields. I could hardly wait for it to begin.[12]

School started out real good [his second year]. The teacher said he could tell I'd been studying because I read better than the others. Going through the woods on the way home that evening, seemed like I was so full of myself I didn't know what to do. I run, and jumped, and kicked, and felt all bouncy, like a ball.[13]

Boys, you are going through a hard country. You have guns and ammunition. Take my advice; anything you see as big as a blackbird, kill it and eat it.[14]

It was the latter end of April when we entered upon an extensive valley at the northwest extremity of the Sierra range. . . . Swarms of wild geese and ducks were swimming on the surface of the cool crystal stream, which was the central fork of the Rio de las Plumas, or sailed the air in clouds over our heads. Dear and antelope filled the plains, and their boldness was conclusive that the hunter's rifle was to them unknown. We struck across this beautiful valley to the waters of the Yuba. . . . We also found gold, but not in sufficient quantity to warrant our working it. . . .[15]

Starting to cross the desert to Black Rock at 4 o'clock in the evening, we traveled all night. The next day it was hot and sandy. . . . A great number of cattle perished before we got to Black Rock. I drove our oxen all the time and I knew about how much an ox could stand. Between nine and ten o'clock a breeze came up and oxen threw up their heads and seemed to have new life. We crossed the South Pass on the Fourth of July. The ice next morning was as thick as a dinner plate.[16]

We left there for Nicodemus, travelling overland with horses and wagons. We were two days on the way, with no roads to direct us save deer trails and buffalo wallows. We travelled by compass. At night the men built bonfires and sat around them, firing guns to keep the wild animals from coming near. We reached Nicodemus about 3 o'clock on the second day.[17]

There is no money in the bank & so very little in town. I saw in the paper tonight that "It was reported that there was a man in town today with fifty cents in currency" but, the editor said, "I don't believe it." Oh! Pa, what are we to do?[18]

Several days before the plague of grasshoppers, my father and his hired man, Jake, came home from the near-by village with tales of trains that could not start or stop because the tracks were slick with crushed grasshoppers. So thick were the grasshoppers that the sun could scarcely be seen.[19]

We went down the river Deschutes in an open canoe, including all the children; and when we got down, there was no way to get to the place where my father had determined to locate us, but to wade through the tremendous swamps. I knew some of the young men that were along laughed at us girls, my oldest sister and me, for holding up what dresses we had to keep from miring; but we did not think it was funny. We finally waded through and got all our goods.[20]

. . . I shall claim to be the smallest boy whose arrow was ever carried away by a moose . . . I gathered myself into a bunch, all ready to spring. As the long-legged beast pulled himself dripping out of the water and shook off the drops from his long hair, I sprang to my feet. I felt some of the water in my face! I gave him my sharpest arrow with all the force I could master, right among the floating ribs. Then I uttered my war whoop.[21]

We could go down to the orchard, where all summer long there were ripe apples and pears, or we could shed our shoes and wade in the San Gabriel . . . We could watch hundreds of pigeons flying in and out of the deserted adobe ranch house . . . or we could go to our retreat in an enlarged coyote hole in the pasture on the other side of the hill. Luckily we did not find any rattlesnakes sharing it with us. We could play in the old stagecoach left in the weeds outside the fence. It remained from earlier days, when it carried the mails, express, and passengers between San Diego, Los Angeles, and San Francisco.[22]

The ceiling of our cabin was usually covered with canvas—in this dirt would collect, making it sag in places, and where the rain or snow had dried, there would be designs on the roof. Mountain rats also made their nests just on top of the canvas and this would make a big sag. Once a rat ran along the canvas and Mama saw the shape of his body and stuck a fork into him. The blood dripped through, and I cried, not because I was sorry for the rat, but just at the sordidness of it all. Then I go out on the hillside, throw myself down flat on my back, and stare straight up at the sky, with such a feeling of relief, knowing that nothing dirty will drop into my eyes.[23]

The mesa was our playground. This mesa is one of the places I love. On top it is rather flat, the ground covered with white daisies; a lovely grove of quaking aspen, fringed on the outside with pines; the trail winding up one side across the top, and down again. . . . at the head of the trail was a tiny grave, and very often I would stop and rest here, reading the baby's name.[24]

The middle room was for the rest of the children to sleep in. Our bed ticks were filled with hay, and when freshly filled smelled so minty. They scratched your arms when stirring them up. In the spring when they are emptied the hay is a fine dust, and smells far from minty.[25]

My God and my mother live in the West, and I will not leave them. It is a tradition of my people that we must never cross the three rivers—the Grande, the San Juan, and the Colorado. Nor could I leave the Chuska Mountains. I was born there. I shall remain. I have nothing to lose but my life, and that they can come and take whenever they please, but I will not move.[26]

Whose voice was first sounded on this land? The voice of the red people who had but bows and arrows. . . . What has been done in my country I did not want, did not ask for it; white people going through my country. . . . When the white man comes to my country he leaves a trail of blood behind him. . . . [27]

I was born upon the prairie, where the wind blew free and there was nothing to break the light of the sun. I was born where there were no enclosures and where everything drew a free breath. I want to die there and not within walls. I know every stream and every wood between the Rio Grande and the Arkansas. I have hunted and lived over that country. I lived like my fathers before me, and like them, I lived happily.[28]

You have driven away our game and our means of livelihood out of the country, until now we have nothing left that is valuable except the hills that you ask us to give up. . . . The earth is full of minerals of all kinds, and on earth the ground is covered with forests of heavy pine, and when we give these up to the Great Father we know that we give up the last thing that is valuable either to us or the white people.[29]

Shall I give the land which is part of my body and leave myself poor and destitute? . . . I cannot say so.[30]

I want no blood upon my land to stain the grass. I want it clear and pure, and I want it so that all who go through among my people may find peace when they come in and leave it when they go out.[31]

We are part of the earth and it is part of us. The perfumed flowers are our sisters; the deer, the horse, the great eagle, these are our brothers. The rocky crests, the flowers in the meadows, the body heat of the pony, and man—all belong to the same family.[32]

The Sioux was a true lover of nature. He loved the earth and all things of the earth. Their tepees were built upon the earth. The birds that flew in the air come to rest upon the earth and it was the final abiding-place of all things that lived and grew. . . . Kinship with all creatures of the earth, sky, and water was a real and active (belief). . . . [33]

Our land is more valuable than your money. It will not even perish by the flames of fire. As long as the sun shines, and the waters flow, this land will be here to give life to men and animals. We cannot sell the lives of men and animals, therefore, we cannot sell this land. It was put here for us by the Great Spirit and we cannot sell it because it does not belong to us.[34]

My father sent for me. I saw he was dying. He said, "My son, my body is returning to my mother earth. . . . This country holds your father's body. Never sell the bones of your father and your mother." My father smiled and passed away. . . . I buried him in that beautiful valley of winding waters. I loved that land more than all the rest of the world. A man who would not love his father's grave is worse than a wild animal.[35]

Endnotes

1. Elinore Pruitt Stewart, *Letters of a Woman Homesteader* (Lincoln: University of Nebraska Press, 1961), 6.

2. John Mack Faragher, *Women and Men on the Overland Trail* (New Haven, Conn.: Yale University Press, 1979), 169.

3. *Ibid.*, 175.

4. Lillian Schlissel, Byrd Gibbens, and Elizabeth Hampsten, *Far From Home: Families of the Westward Journey* (New York: Schocken Books, 1989), 157.

5. *Ibid.*, 177.

6. *Ibid.*, 112.

7. *Eyewitnesses and Others, Volume 1* (New York: Holt, Rinehart, and Winston, 1991), 296-7.

8. Paula Bartley and Cathy Loxton, *Plains Women: Women in the American West* (Cambridge, Mass.: Cambridge University Press, 1991), 10.

9. Christiane Fischer, ed., *Let Them Speak for Themselves: Women in the American West, 1849-1900* (Hamden, Conn.: The Shoe String Press, 1977), 42-43.

10. Robert G. Athearn, *In Search of Canaan: Black Migration to Kansas, 1879-80* (Lawrence: The Regents Press of Kansas, 1978), 80.

11. *Ibid.*, 84.

12. *Eyewitnesses and Others, Volume 2* (New York: Holt, Rinehart, and Winston, 1991), 248.

13. *Ibid.*

14. William Loren Katz, *Eyewitness: The Negro in American History* (New York: Pitman Publishing Corporation, 1969), 75.

15. *Ibid.*, 90.

16. *Ibid.*, 90-91.

17. Bartley and Loxton, *Plains Women*, 16.

18. Schlissel, Gibbens, and Hampsten, *Far From Home*, 135.

19. *Eyewitnesses and Others, Volume 2*, 56.

20. Russell Freedman, *Children of the West* (New York: Clarion Books, 1983), 26.

21. *Ibid.*, 42.

22. *Ibid.*, 83.

23. Anne Ellis, *The Life of an Ordinary Woman* (New York: Houghton Mifflin Company, 1929), 42.

24. *Ibid.*, 61-62.

25. *Ibid.*, 81.

26. Dee Brown, *Bury My Heart at Wounded Knee* (New York: Bantam Books, 1970), 32.

27. *Ibid.*, 101.

28. *Ibid.*, 236.

29. *Ibid.*

30. Angie Debo, *A History of the Indians of the United States* (Norman: University of Oklahoma Press, 1970), 157.

31. *Ibid.*, 219.

32. "Our Family With the Earth," *Cobblestone* 10, no. 8 (August 1989): 22.

33. Derek Wise, *The American West* (New York: Macmillan, 1984), 10.

34. *Ibid.*, 11.

35. *Ibid.*

2 Trade Routes in the Old Northwest—1790-1850

Cameron Buckland, Shaker Heights High School, Shaker Heights, Ohio

Grade Level/Subject: Eleventh Grade—U. S. History

NCSS Thematic Strands:

❷ TIME, CONTINUITY, AND CHANGE (High School)

b. apply key concepts such as time, chronology, causality, change, conflict, and complexity to explain, analyze, and show connections among patterns of historical change and continuity; and

d. systematically employ processes of critical historical inquiry to reconstruct and reinterpet the past, such as using a variety of sources and checking for their credibility, validating and weighing evidence for claims, and searching for causality.

❸ PEOPLE, PLACES, AND ENVIRONMENTS (High School)

a. refine mental maps of locales, regions, and the world that demonstrate understanding of relative location, direction, size, and shape;

b. create, interpret, use, and synthesize information from various representations of the earth, such as maps, globes, and photographs;

d. calculate distance, scale, area, and density, and distinguish spatial distribution patterns;

e. describe, differentiate, and explain the relationships among various regional and global patterns of geographic phenomena such as landforms, soils, climate, vegetation, natural resources, and population; and

f. use knowledge of physical system changes such as seasons, climate and weather, and the water cycle to explain geographic phenomena.

❼ PRODUCTION, DISTRIBUTION, AND CONSUMPTION (High School)

a. explain how the scarcity of productive resources (human, capital, technological, and natural) requires the development of economic systems to make decisions about how goods and services are to be produced and distributed;

b. analyze the role that supply and demand, prices, incentives, and profits play in determining what is produced and distributed in a competitive market system;

e. analyze the role of specialization and exchange in economic processes; and

h. apply economic concepts and reasoning when evaluating historical and contemporary social developments and issues.

Key Features of Powerful Teaching and Learning

Integrative—the lesson combines major concepts from geography (e.g., location, physical features, and spatial relationships) and economics (e.g., specialization, scarcity, and interdependence) in a history lesson. Students discover historical generalizations that are as applicable to the student's world of today as they were during the early 1800s. For example, youngsters learn (a) to appreciate the adage that necessity is the mother of invention and (b) to understand that a successful entrepreneur must be able to adapt to changing economic and societal conditions;

Challenging—student groups critically analyze and organize evidence to identify the strengths and weaknesses of various trade routes. Then each group engages in reflective inquiry about trading activities by (a) formulating and asking a set of questions and (b) evaluating the answers to those questions; and

Active—each student is encouraged to ask both factual and inquiry type questions about trade routes during the 1820s. These questions are to be in a "yes" or "no" form and are to be answered by the teacher. This format forces students to engage in reflective inquiry rather than depending on the teacher to tell them what and how to think. Each student will keep a data sheet of all relevant points that are made during the classwide questioning phase. Then, during the group phase, students engage in cooperative learning by refining and sharing their knowledge about each travel route.

Purpose/Rationale/Introduction

This lesson is designed to enable students to understand the development of the North Central region—the area from the Appalachians to the Mississippi River—between 1800 and 1840. Specifically, each student group analyzes the actions of a mythical trader in Fort Recovery, Ohio—who wishes to ship his produce, ten tons of corn and wheat, to New York City during the fall of 1820—by examining reflectively four routes that were used by traders. The students are to determine which route and what methods of transportation on that route would have enabled the trader to maximize his profit.

In addition, the lesson results in many types of tangential learning. For example, as students examine each route, they learn the location of many cities and physical features as well as the interaction that occurs between these geographical factors. They also develop the ability to think like an entrepreneur as they assess the economic potential of each route. Finally, students recognize many cause and effect relationships and thus learn to appreciate the importance of chronology.

Objectives (Students will):

a. identify the various methods of transportation used between 1790 and 1850;

b. describe why transportation methods used between 1790 and 1850 changed dramatically;

c. explain why different sections of the nation depended on different methods of transportation;

d. determine why water transportation was usually more efficient than land transportation;

e. analyze how physical features affected travel;

f. discriminate between economically productive and unproductive trade routes;

g. describe the myriad of problems faced by the transporters;

h. recognize that economic activities involve a series of choices;

i. accept that producers who pick the most viable choices are rewarded economically;

j. propose the idea that when producers are free to innovate, economic efficiency is usually increased;

k. synthesize historical evidence gathered by the use of inquiry methods in a cooperative learning situation; and

l. evaluate the economic viability of various patterns and methods of transportation.

Time Allotment: three, fifty-minute class sessions

Resources Needed

1. one or more large classroom maps depicting the United States during the early 1800s (one map must include physical features);

2. a map that depicts the Great Lakes area around 1820. (Note: If an instructor is able to provide students with access to a series of maps that depict the economic development of the United States between 1790 and 1850, students will be more likely to discover and analyze changes that occurred during this period.);

3. several optional textbooks, a set of encyclopedias, and several library books that contain a section about the western development of the United States between 1790 and 1850;

4. the map of major U.S. trade routes (circa. 1840) included with this lesson plan (see appendix); and

5. computer resources, depending on the expertise of the class and the technology that is available.

Procedure

Description of the Four Routes

1. From Fort Recovery (located in northwest Ohio), then across the Great Lakes (Erie and Ontario), then across upstate New York to Albany, and finally, south to New York City via the Hudson River.

2. From Fort Recovery east across Ohio by land to Wheeling and/or Pittsburgh, then across the Appalachians to eastern Pennsylvania, then by land across New Jersey to New York City.

3. From Fort Recovery south around the Appalachians to Atlanta, then north along the East Coast (students must decide to follow either a land or water route when they travel along the east side of the Appalachians).

4. From Fort Recovery west to the Mississippi River primarily via a water route—first travel over land to Piqua, Ohio; then downstream via the Great Miami River to Cincinnati; then downstream via the Ohio River to the Mississippi River at Cairo, Illinois. Then continue on downstream via the Mississippi River to New Orleans, and finally, travel via the Gulf of Mexico and the Atlantic Ocean to New York City.

Class Preparation

Begin by describing the inquiry problem to each class. It is suggested that a map depicting the four routes (see appendix) be provided to each student to stimulate interest. Make sure each student traces (with a highlighter) each route on his or her copy of the map.

Each student should be told to read an assignment that covers the development of internal improvements in the United States between 1790 and 1850 (any standard text can be used). Then each student should form four or five questions that the student believes will provide him or her with clues that will enable him or her to solve the problem. Each question should be able to be answered with a "yes" or "no" response.

The teacher needs to be certain that several resources are available to help students engage in productive classroom research (see materials listed in the resource section).

Day One

Tell each student to divide a sheet of paper in half—label one column the Yes column and the other the No column. The teacher should ask each student to ask one question that he or she most wants answered.

Examples of the type of questions typically posed include (a) Was the Erie Canal completed? (b) Were steamboats used on the Ohio and Mississippi Rivers? (c) Were clipper ships used on the Great Lakes? and (d) Was there a paved roadway through the Appalachians?

The teacher responds to each of these initial questions with a "yes" or "no" response—the student should be encouraged to ask one or two follow-up "yes" or "no" type questions that are designed to help clarify and amplify the first answer. The object of the follow-up questions is to engage the students in reflective inquiry by encouraging the construction of sensible inferences based on the answers to the original "yes" or "no" questions. This aspect of the learning activity should take about one minute per student.

Following this initial inquiry phase, any student who wishes to ask another question should be given the chance. The instructor needs to make certain all students are allowed to pose follow-up questions to these questions. This encourages students to evaluate previous questions and to test and modify any hypotheses they have begun to form.

Day Two

Students are placed in groups (generally three to six students seems to work best). Explain that each group is expected to develop a hypothesis based on Day One's findings as well as on research that group members will complete from the various resources that are available in the classroom. Allow each group to ask any "yes" or "no" question that (a) remains from its original lists, (b) was formulated during the previous day's work, or (c) develops based on the groups' research. The teacher must make certain that research continues as the teacher circulates from group to group to answer students' inquiries. After approximately forty minutes, the teacher should present each group with a final form to be filled out on Day Three (see appendix).

For the remainder of the period, the teacher can answer each group's questions about the manner in which members will complete their response. The teacher should try to make certain that each group understands that it must (a) choose the route it believes a trader would be most likely to use successfully and (b) identify the several forms of transportation the trader would have used to transport the goods most efficiently.

Day Three

Inform the class that each group's final answer is due at the end of the period (if desired, groups may be allowed to turn in the final answer at the beginning of the next day). Reiterate that each group must fill in the form in a manner that clearly shows (a) the precise route the group picks, (b) the places where there will be changes in transportation methods, and (c) the types of transportation that will be used during each step of the trip. Any research that students conduct this day should be kept to a minimum to ensure that students concentrate on clearly and precisely delineating their final response.

Assessment

Each student group's answers on the Final Response Form (see appendix) will be graded based on three criteria: (1) the amount of time the group's trip would take, (2) the dollar amount of goods that could be transported by the methods each group selects, and (3) the probability of successfully completing the trip dependent on the route chosen by each group.

A teacher might decide to provide a copy of each response to every group. If so, the teacher should instruct each group to evaluate each group's responses. Thus, students would learn to evaluate various answers and then to compare those responses to their own.

In addition to evaluating each group's response, it is critically important to assess each individual's knowledge. To do this, a teacher might ask each student to apply his or her knowledge to a novel situation by writing a short essay noting how and why in Ohio in 1998 (or in any other state) products are transported by different routes and methods to the East Coast than the methods used in this exercise. An instructor could also include a similar application type question in future units that includes revolutionary transportation changes on diverse topics such as the development of canals and railroads, development of the interstate highway system and the trucking industry, and, finally, the development of ocean shipping in the Great Lakes as a result of the opening of the St. Lawrence Seaway.

Collectively, these assessment techniques enable a teacher to determine both if each student understands the material presented in the unit and can apply key concepts and principles from this unit in novel situations.

Extended Rationale

This interdisciplinary inquiry lesson extensively uses knowledge drawn from the disciplines of history, economics, and geography. Any route except number 3 (south around the Appalachians) offered traders the opportunity to make money depending on the precise methods of transportation chosen.

It is generally acknowledged, however, that the most economically viable journey entailed the following: (a) travel from Fort Recovery to Piqua, Ohio, by Connestoga wagon; (b) then travel downstream by raft on the Miami River to Cincinnati; (c) then travel downstream by keelboat to Louisville (steamboat travel upstream from Louisville was unreliable); (c) then travel on a steamboat to New Orleans, and, finally; (e) travel across the Gulf of Mexico and the Atlantic Ocean on a clipper ship.

Although few student groups precisely identify both this route and these means of transportation as the most profitable, other routes and methods afforded a trader nearly as much opportunity to profit. Thus, other student responses can be considered accurate provided the students have logically chosen and documented a reasoned response.

As a result of the reflective thinking that students engage in during this exercise, they become much more familiar with several major concepts in history, economics, and geography. For example, change is the essential concept that unifies history—and students repeatedly encounter this concept during the lesson. Students discover that transportation methods changed rapidly between 1800 and 1840 (e.g., the completion of the Erie Canal in 1825 made route #1 much more economically viable, while the development of railroads during the 1830s made travel across the Appalachians [route #2] much more efficient).

In addition, most groups relate their answers to cultural interactions that occurred between Native Americans and pioneers—a factor that increases student interest in the Native American forced removal during the Jacksonian period. Finally, students usually gain a unique perspective on the development of sectionalism through the study of the economic ties that developed between the Northeast and the old Northwest.

During the exercise, students gain knowledge of critically important economic concepts that center on the role that scarcity played in helping to develop the frontier. In solving the problem, most youngsters gain appreciation for (a) the role specialization plays in economic activities, (b) the manner in which supply and demand affects market forces, and (c) the manner in which interdependence contributes to economic productivity. Collectively, these insights enable students to realize how individual freedom of choice contributed to both economic efficiency and growth during the early and middle 1800s.

The important role that place name geography occupies in this exercise seems obvious. But students engage in much more than merely place name geography. Although presenting them with an intriguing problem does seem to help many less able students develop increased proficiency in remembering place names and locations in the eastern United States, much more importantly, spatial relationship skills are refined when students analyze how diverse physical features affected westerners' economic activities.

Extension and Enrichment
After students turn in their final response, they can be given the chance to apply their new knowledge to events they have experienced in their own lives. Extra points can be given to students who reflectively apply their knowledge to relevant modern day examples and then write a page or two that accurately analyzes similarities between their example and the Fort Recovery exercise.

Resources
Bragdon, Henry W., and Samuel P. McCutchen. *History of a Free People*. New York: The Macmilllan Company, 1964.

Appendix

Final Response Form—Fort Recovery to New York City Exercise

State the route you believe the trader should take. Note the method you believe the trader will choose from Fort Recovery to the trader's first stop. Then note each place where the type of transportation used would change—make certain you also note the new form of transportation that would be used. You may make as many as TEN changes during the trip. Be as precise as possible in completing each of the THREE columns.

Location		Location		Method of Transportation
1. Fort Recovery	to		by	
2.	to		by	
3.	to		by	
4.	to		by	
5.	to		by	
6.	to		by	
7.	to		by	
8.	to		by	
9.	to		by	
10.	to		by	

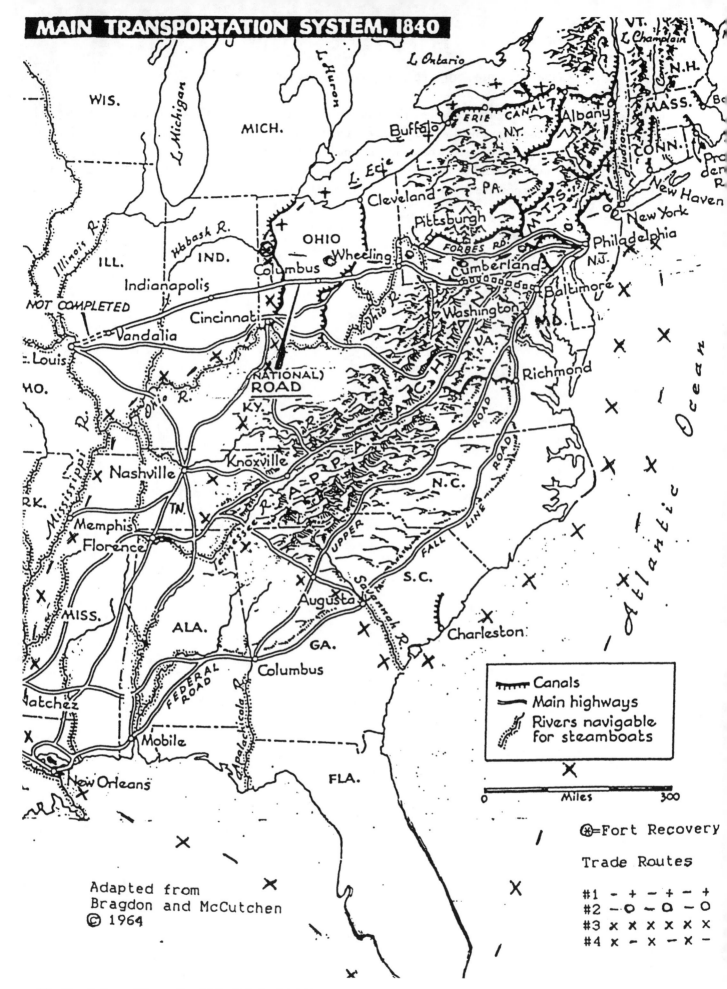

MAIN TRANSPORTATION SYSTEM, 1840

WIS.

L. Michigan

MICH.

L. Huron

L. Ontario

VT.
L. Champlain
N.H.

ILL.

Hubash R.

IND.

OHIO

L. Erie

Buffalo
ERIE CANAL
N.Y.
Albany

MASS.

Illinois R.

Indianapolis

Columbus

Wheeling

Cleveland

PA.

Pittsburgh

MTS.

CONN.

Pro-
den-
R.

New Haven

New York

Philadelphia

N.J.

NOT COMPLETED

Vandalia

Cincinnati

NATIONAL
ROAD

FORBES RD.

Cumberland

Baltimore

MD.

St. Louis

Ohio R.

KY.

Ohio R.

Washington

VA.

Richmond

A
P
P
A
L
A
C
H
I

ROAD

MO.

Nashville

Knoxville

N.C.

Atlantic Ocean

RK.

Mississippi R.

Memphis
Florence

TN.

Tennessee R.

A
N

R.

UPPER

FALL LINE ROAD

S.C.

MISS.

ALA.

Columbus

GA.

Augusta

Savannah R.

Charleston

FEDERAL ROAD

Apalachicola R.

Natchez

Mobile

New Orleans

FLA.

Legend

⌇⌇⌇	Canals
—	Main highways
⌇	Rivers navigable for steamboats

×

0 — Miles — 300

⊛=Fort Recovery

Trade Routes

#1 – + – + – +
#2 – 0 – 0 – 0
#3 × × × × × ×
#4 × – × – × –

Adapted from
Bragdon and McCutchen
© 1964

Surveying Japanese Students: Comparing Students from Different Cultures*

William P. Fitzhugh, Reisterstown Elementary School, Reisterstown, Maryland

Grade Level/Subject: Grades 3-5—Social Studies
This lesson can also be used with middle school students.

NCSS Thematic Strands:

❶ CULTURE
a. explore and describe similarities and differences in the way groups, societies, and cultures address similar human needs and concerns.

⓸ INDIVIDUAL DEVELOPMENT AND IDENTITY
f. explore factors that contribute to one's personal identity such as interests, capabilities, and perceptions.

Purpose/Rationale/Introduction
In this series of activities, students will display data from a questionnaire completed by a selected class of Japanese elementary school students. The class will then complete the same questionnaire themselves. The students will tally results from both questionnaires and display data in an appropriate form: a graph or possibly a Venn diagram. The students will compare the results of the Japanese questionnaire with their own questionnaire and discover similarities and differences between their culture and the Japanese culture. The Japanese students polled live in Hiroshima, a Japanese city comparable in size to Baltimore.

Objectives
Students will:

a. learn information about the daily lives of Japanese children their own age;

b. draw conclusions about the similarities and differences between their own lives and the lives of students from another country and culture;

c. gain an understanding and appreciation for another culture;

d. use graphing skills to analyze and appropriately display results of both questionnaires; and

e. be able to complete a questionnaire about themselves.

Time Allotment:
This social studies lesson can be correlated with graphing skills taught in mathematics class. Using both social studies and math periods, a teacher and class can complete these activities over a span of three days or six class periods.

---

* *This article has been reprinted from* Tora No Maki II: Lessons for Teaching about Contemporary Japan *(Washington, D.C. and Bloomington, Ind.: National Council for the Social Studies and ERIC Clearinghouse for Social Studies/Social Science Education, 1997), 35-39.*

Resources Needed

1. graph paper for different kinds of graphs;
2. writing paper;
3. drawing paper; and
4. Appendices 1-3: Student questionnaire to be completed by the class; data display of answers from Japanese student questionnaire; and notes for teachers to accompany questionnaire results.

Procedure

1. Students will complete a questionnaire about themselves. Teacher will discuss the nature of answering questions about their likes and dislikes. Students should be cautioned about doing their own work and not discussing responses. After completion the teacher will collect questionnaires.

2. Teacher will divide class into small groups of students. These groups will be assigned several questions from the questionnaire. Students will tally the results of their section of the questionnaire. The tallied results from the questionnaire will be displayed for the entire class.

3. Each small group will determine which graph (pictograph, pie chart, bar graph, line graph) of its data will be most suitable and make a graph for each of the questions in their section of the questionnaire's data. Students will make a graph for each set of student responses. There will be two graphs (one for Japan, one for the U.S.) for each question. Note: Teachers should determine before beginning that students know how to graph data. This can serve as an integrated math/social studies lesson.

4. Small groups of students will tally the data in Appendix 2 from the corresponding questions they completed from their own class's questionnaire responses. They will then use the same kind of graphs (used in their own survey) to graph the Japanese student data.

5. In their small groups, students will orally compare and contrast the results of specific questions from the questionnaire. Students will look for similarities and differences in the responses. Students will use vocabulary such as: "greater than," "less than," and "equal to." Students will look for ways to combine sections of graph data.

6. Each student will write a paragraph expressing the inferences found in "5."

Assessment

1. Teacher will assess the conclusions drawn by the groups concerning the similarities and differences each group has compiled from its section of the questionnaire.

2. Teacher will assign a written question about the similarities and differences of specific questionnaire questions to the class.

3. Teacher will assign a written question about the results regarding the similarities and differences each student can find from examining the responses from both Japan and the U.S. questionnaire.

4. Individual students can complete a Venn diagram using graphing data as a source material.

Extension and Enrichment

1. Students can make their graphs on large poster board to display their own class results with Japanese student results. These can be hung in the school foyer.

2. Another class can complete the survey. Students from each class can compare their own class responses with those of another or compare the new class with the Japanese class. Are there marked differences between American classes or between the second American class and the Japanese class?

3. Students can use this data about themselves to write an autobiography or make an "All About Me" book.

Student Questionaire

1. I live in _____

2. I was born in _____

3. On my vacation, I went to _____

4. My favorite sport to play is _____

5. My favorite sport to watch is _____

6. When I grow up my job will be _____

7. My favorite food is _____

8. My favorite color is _____

9. My birthmonth is _____

10. My favorite subject in school is _____

11. My least favorite subject in school is _____

12. My pet at home is _____

13. My hobbies are _____

14. My favorite TV show is _____

15. My favorite holiday is _____

16. My favorite season of the year is _____

17. People in my family (including me) are _____

Appendix 2

Data Display of Answers from Japanese Student Questionnaire

1. *"I live in ..."*
   Hiroshima-31

2. *"I was born in ..."*
   Hiroshima-25, Osaka-2, Yamaguchi-2, Goto-retto-1, Kyoto-1

3. *"On vacation I went to ..."*
   pool-3, camp-3, home-4, Osaka-3, grandma's-2, Nara-1, hotel-2, Tokyo-1, Spaceworld-1, Shikoku-1, sea-6, mountains-2

4. *"My favorite sport to play is ..."*
   rope skipping-2, swimming-5, badminton-2, baseball-10, soccer-7, basketball-2, running-2

5. *"My favorite sport to watch is ..."*
   soccer-4, baseball-19, volleyball-1, swimming-1

6. *"When I grow up my job will be ..."*
   millionaire-1, soccer player-5, carpenter-1, baseball player-4, nurse-1, teacher-5, building superintendent-1, cartoonist-2, train driver-1, store clerk (bakery, retail, florist, clothing)-6

7. *"My favorite food is ..."*
   everything-1, meat (includes steak, yakitori)-8, sweets-1, fish (includes sushi)-3, pizza-1, hamburger-5, okonomiyaki (cabbage-based pancakes)-2, curry-1, ramen noodles-1, cake-1, gratin-1, rice-1, tempura (fried seafood and vegetables)-1, watermelon-1, spaghetti-1,

8. *"My favorite color is ..."*
   blue-7, sky blue-5, purple-7, pink-4, silver-1, white-1, yellow-1, red-1, green-1

9. *"My birth month is ..."*
   January-3, February-5, March-5, April-0, May-2, June-3, July-4, August-1, September-2, October-1, November-2, December-1

10. *"My favorite subject in school is ..."*
    art-7, math-5, gym-10, social studies-2, science-2, language-2, music-2, nothing-1

11. *"My least favorite subject in school is ..."*
    math-8, sociology-5, language-6, swimming-2, art-4, gym-1, music-2, nothing disliked-5

12. *"My pet at home is ..."*
    tropical fish-8, dog-3, insect-1, hamster-1, bird-4, rabbit-1, cat-1, crayfish-1, no pet-11

13. *"My hobbies are ..."*
    reading-10, playing-7, family time-7, drawing-4, soccer-3,

14. *"My favorite TV show is ..."*
    Magical Zunou Power (game show)-5, Conan (children's animation)-6, Tomei Ningen (teen drama)-1, Crayon Shin Chan (children's animation)-1, Bakusou Kyodai (boys' animation)-1, Kaitou Saint Tale (girls' animation)-2, Dragon Ball (children's animation)-3, Mokuyou No Kaidan (horror)-1

15. *"My favorite holidays are ..."*
    summer school holiday-21, spring school holiday-8, winter school holiday-1, New Year's-1

16. *"My favorite season of the year is ..."*
    all-4, summer-10, winter-4, spring-10, fall-3

17. *"People in my family (including me) are ..."*
    three-2, four-15, five-2, six-3

Appendix 3

Notes for Teachers to Accompany Questionnaire Results

The ideas below are presented to facilitate discussion of the corresponding responses to the questionnaire.

1. Many students at one school have different city/town mailing addresses.
2. Locate the birthplaces of students. Map the out-of-state and in-state sites. Were any of your students born outside the U.S.?
3. Ask your students for specific places or place names like Denver, not generalities such as camp or pool.
4. Find maps of playgrounds, baseball diamonds, etc. to display to students. Brainstorm for equipment needed for each sport.
5. A number of students mentioned Hiroshima Carp or Tokyo Giants. Locate American baseball teams on your U.S. Map.
6. Which jobs need a college education? Which jobs provide goods and services?
7. Which are "Western" foods? Sort foods according to your food pyramid. Try cooking some of these foods with your class—yum!
8. Try to discover why each color choice was significant for your students. Which colors do children of both cultures like?
9. Showa refers to a year in the reign of the late Emperor Hirohito. We sometimes refer to the presidency of . . . What other ways are there of demarcating time?
10. What is sociology?
11. Will students use "nothing disliked" in their graphs? This is student decision making. Most schools in Japan have outdoor swimming pools!
12. Only 1 cat! This is unusual; cats are said to bring good luck in Japan. What kinds of things do animals represent in our culture? What other things are symbols of good luck in our culture?
13. Sort these according to activity level.
14. Most Japanese children like cartoons which are also extremely popular with adults, too. Categorize the type of programming your students prefer.
15. Japanese children attend school 240 days a year. Their school calendar is much different from ours.
16. Summers are hot and humid, and there is a rainy season from mid-June to mid-July. Describe the seasonal weather where you live. Look up the daily weather report for Tokyo.
17. How do sizes of families differ between the two cultures? Traditionally, Japanese tended to be more likely to live with their extended families. What does this mean?

The Culture of Native Americans

Larry Fontanarosa, Frank Ohl Middle School, Austintown Local Schools, Youngstown, Ohio

Grade Level/Subject: Eighth Grade—U. S. History

NCSS Thematic Strands:

❶ CULTURE

c. describe ways in which language, stories, folktales, music, and artistic creations serve as expressions of culture and influence behavior of people living in a particular culture (Early Grades);

b. explain how information and experiences may be interpreted by people from diverse cultural perspectives and frames of reference (Middle Grades); and

f. interpret patterns of behavior reflecting values and attitudes that contribute or pose obstacles to cross-cultural understanding (High School).

Key Features of Powerful Teaching and Learning

Meaningful—a variety of learning activities that involve the aural and visual senses, and Native American artifacts, are used to encourage an appreciation and understanding of Native American culture;

Integrative—students are encouraged to reflect on the past through a current perspective. They are also encouraged to make contact with Native American populations through the Internet;

Challenging—this inquiry lesson has roots in auditory and visual stimulation, group activities, and group discussions. These exercises permit students to develop new understanding about their previously held beliefs while collecting evidence from multiple sources. Students form concluding generalizations about the plight of Native Americans; and

Active—many students have preconceived ideas about Native American people. Because bias may exist for many reasons, this lesson will allow students to test their beliefs through several activities, many of which involve interactive discourse. This lesson is intended to be the spark that stimulates each student to begin actively constructing knowledge in his or her search for truth about people from cultures dissimilar to his or her own.

Purpose/Rationale/Introduction

The Native Americans were living in America when the nation expanded through exploration. Although different Native American nations existed, they were culturally joined by shared beliefs. According to Compton's Interactive Encyclopedia, one belief was that "Indians believed in a supernatural force which pervaded all nature." In a society that experienced an "Age of Reason" and witnessed major scientific findings such as those of Benjamin Franklin, the general culture in America was quite different from that of Native Americans. Considering the marked differences between these two cultures, it is understandable that the Native American way of life may have threatened American expansion.

Objectives (Students will):

a. construct new knowledge about the plight of Native Americans by building on previous knowledge;

b. identify factors that contributed to the near extinction of Native Americans;

c. draw conclusions about the importance of effective communication among people from dissimilar cultures;

d. infer reasons that people from dissimilar cultures may have different views;

e. complete writing journals;

f. experience listening skills through group projects;

g. participate in group discussion;

h. practice critical thinking skills; and

i. reflect on new experiences.

Time Allotment: two, fifty minute class periods

Resources Needed

Dictionary, note cards with symbols that represent the letters of the alphabet (see appendix), *Keepers of the Earth* book, arrowheads, dream catchers, medicine wheels, sweet grass, filmstrip depicting the struggles of Native Americans during westward expansion by settlers, filmstrip projector, compact disc player, "Indian Reservation (The Lament of the Cherokee Reservation Indian)" on compact disc performed by The Raiders, "It Is a Good Day to Die" on compact disc performed by Robbie Robertson and the Red Ensemble, chalk, crayons, pencils, 4"x 2' strips of paper.

Procedure

Read the definition of communication aloud to the students. Next, add brief comments to enhance the meaning. Then, allow the students to arrange their own groups of four. Discuss the importance of effective communication among people at home, school, and in society. Continue the discussion with results of ineffective communication.

Read the story "Gluscabi and the Wind Eagle" (*Keepers of the Earth*) to the students. This Native American legend is about a young boy who can communicate with an eagle he calls his grandfather. According to the legend, wind is a result of the grandfather's flapping his wings. One day the eagle is captured by a hunter and is unable to flap his wings. Gluscabi notices that there must be trouble because it is a very hot day and surely grandfather would provide wind for comfort. Gluscabi searches for his grandfather and finds him in a crevice with his wings tied. After freeing his grandfather and unbinding his wings, grandfather replies, "Grandson, I hear what you say. "

Stimulate the group sharing process by asking, "Does this story reflect effective communication?" Students share their prior knowledge with the group by responding to this question and also construct a cognitive bridge to what they know. Visit each group of students while members are interacting to get a feel for student background knowledge.

Students remain in groups and imagine they are representatives from a distant planet. Students name their planet to reflect a holiday custom unique to their planet and speak a language only they can understand. The language is determined by each student's randomly picking from a hat a note card with symbols representing the alphabet. Students walk among classmates and inform them about family customs for the upcoming holiday using only their coded language. Encourage students to relay their customs by nonverbal communication. This may include written symbols and reading body language; however, these are not inclusive. Effective communication usually includes more than spoken words. Teachers should add some humor to this lesson for those who are experiencing dissonance. This can be done by using their own codes to get everyone in the room involved. Once students witness the teacher's involvement, they may become more likely to participate. Students verbally report their individual translations to the class while incorporating historical imagination to place themselves in the Native American's predicament of communication with people who spoke a different language.

Students have their visual and auditory senses stimulated by viewing a filmstrip depicting the struggles of Native Americans during westward expansion in America. After introducing the filmstrip, ask students to recall their thoughts about effective communication and look for evidence in the filmstrip to support their ideas.

Stress the importance of writing down evidence from the filmstrip because it can be useful to build future knowledge. Play the filmstrip ("America: Gone West") using the original soundtrack, which supports the position of the U.S. government to remove Native Americans from their land during westward expansion. Next, replay the filmstrip with the soundtrack "It Is a Good Day to Die." It supports Native American culture and portrays the U.S. government as a key element in the near destruction of the Native American people. Encourage students to interact with each other and discuss what they saw. Stress the importance of realizing how the same events can be viewed differently by people of different cultures. Discuss the experiences felt by other cultural groups, such as Italian or Polish Americans in America, similarities with the Native American plight, and their past treatment, which is a large part of the formation of our country. Provide time for questions with "Anything About Anything." This discussion activity allows students to ask any question relevant to the new knowledge they have acquired. To screen questions, have students write their questions on paper to be collected. Also, this allows those who are not comfortable talking to a large group to have their query answered.

Each group focuses on an assigned theme. The idea is to synthesize one "Grand Idea" concerning the Native American plight. Themes include cultural awareness, cultural perspectives, preconceived ideas, and effective communication. Ask groups to display each main idea on a large strip of paper and present it to the class. Next, group members tape their project on the wall to form an arrowhead constructed through the efforts of the whole class.

The culminating activity is to darken the classroom while students listen to "Indian Reservation" (The Lament of the Cherokee Reservation Indian) by The Raiders. After the song, the students write reflective journal entries, which should focus on reasons people from dissimilar cultures view events differently. Evidence collected from the filmstrip should be included to support their positions.

Assessment

Each student demonstrates his or her level of improved awareness and understanding of Native American problems, including language barriers and cultural differences, through a written report. Students are graded according to their degree of understanding three relevant criteria that are reflected in their report: (1) recognition of communication problems, not just for Americans, but for many cultures that have dissimilar languages, values, and customs; (2) explanation of reasons why people from dissimilar cultures may have different views; and (3) identification of factors that contributed to the near extinction of Native Americans. This can be placed in the student's social studies portfolio, and a copy can be placed in the student's language arts portfolio.

Teacher assessment can also be attained through a reflective teacher journal. This single journal kept by the teacher affords him or her the luxury to reflect on teacher and student performance while it is still fresh. It permits the teacher to look into past lessons and helps him or her recall materials for future use. Also, this journal can be read by colleagues to share the experience.

Extension

Heighten the aura of this lesson by inviting Native Americans from your community. All can benefit through effective communication with people from dissimilar cultures. Also, students should be encouraged to apply their new knowledge through technology. This can be easily accomplished by browsing the World Wide Web and the Internet for related topics. Through technology, students can have conversations with Native American students, discuss history, and perhaps make a new friend! 🕸

References

Capps, B. *The Indians*. New York: Time Life Books, 1973.

Catado, M. J., and J. Bruchac. *Keepers of the Earth*. Golden, Colo.: Fulcrum Inc., 1989.

Compton's Interactive Encyclopedia for Windows. [CD ROM]. Carlsbad, Calif.: Compton's News Media, Inc., 1996.

Cooke, A. *America: Gone West* (filmstrip). New York: Time-Life Films, Multi-Media Division, 1973.

Liptak, K. *North American Indian Sign Language*. New York: Scholastic, 1990.

Loudermilk, J. D. "Indian Reservation" (the Lament of the Cherokee Reservation Indian) [Recorded by K. Allison, J. Correro, M. Lindsay, P. Revere, F. Weller, 1963]. *On the Legend of Paul Revere* [CD]. New York: CBS Records, 1990.

Robertson, R. "It Is a Good Day to Die." On *Music for Native Americans* [CD]. Hollywood, Calif.: Capitol Records, 1994.

Touzet, J. S. "The Cherokee Alphabet and Pronunciation Guide." joyce.eng.yale.edu/~jolo/CherTabl.html, 1998.

Symbols

✓ A	♍ F	❖ K	✦ P	✻ U
♌ B	♒ G	⊠ L	✷ Q	℞ V
▫ C	♐ H	⌘ M	⊕ R	← W
◉ D	♓ I	▯ N	✧ S	♈ X
♋ E	◆ J	⊙ O	♌ T	♉ Y
				☯ Z

5 Constantine Village Cemetery—A Bridge to Today

Elvin W. Keith III, Constantine High School, Constantine, Michigan

Grade Level/Subject: Eleventh Grade—U. S. History

NCSS Thematic Strands:

❶ TIME, CONTINUITY, AND CHANGE (High School)

b. apply key concepts such as time, chronology, causality, change, conflict, and complexity to explain, analyze, and show connections among patterns of historical change and continuity; and

d. systematically employ processes of critical historical inquiry to reconstruct and reinterpret the past, such as using a variety of sources and checking their credibility, validating and weighing evidence for claims, and searching for causality.

Key Features of Powerful Teaching and Learning

Meaningful—to many students, U.S. history has little meaning in the "real world" of today. This lesson will help students to connect the past of Constantine village and St. Joseph County to the present citizens and village institutions. Each student engages in an in-depth exploration of a person from the past selected from a cemetery headstone that leads to understanding and appreciation of the past and the present;

Integrative—this lesson will enable students to connect history over time as it relates to our village and area. It integrates past U.S., state, and community history with the present. Learnings from the disciplines of history and English are applied in the development of a required research paper;

Challenging—students will be challenged to use all available school and community resources to obtain information. Each student is encouraged to apply interviewing techniques to obtain personal knowledge of past events from relatives or acquaintances of those being studied; and

Active—this lesson requires students to "do" history rather than simply sit and read history as they engage in the process of historical inquiry. Students actively construct knowledge starting with the moment they record information from their cemetery headstone through the process of investigating sources to writing the final report.

Purpose/Rationale/Introduction

The purpose of this lesson is for students to learn about life in Constantine and St. Joseph County, Michigan, during the lifetime of a selected person from the Constantine village cemetery. Each student will connect a historical time in Constantine with the concurrent historical time in Michigan and the United States. The intention is to tie the study of U.S. history to the place where each student lives. Students will learn that history is "alive" and has relevance to each person and his or her community. Because our community is small and relatively stable, much of what happened in history since the founding of Constantine can still be studied and a clear relationship to modern-day Constantine can be seen.

An additional purpose of this lesson is to bring the local community and the school together. Another reason for this llesson is to make people living in our town aware that Constantine

High School students are learning not just about the United States but also about Constantine as it was and as it is today. Students will learn that the people of Constantine made an important contribution to the history of Michigan and the United States.

Objectives (Students will):

a. relate past Constantine community, St. Joseph's County, and Michigan history to the present day;

b. identify, describe, summarize, and interpret historical events, issues, and other happenings related to the person investigated within his or her historical era;

c. make connections between academic life in school and political, social, and economic life in the community;

d. consult a variety of written and primary sources from school and community resources;

e. interview community persons who may have knowledge of past people, events, etc.; and

f. write a research paper reporting findings.

Time Allotment

Although this project is intended to be a semester experience, the actual classroom instruction time is limited to one period of teacher-led orientation on the goals of the project and specific instruction on how the tasks are to be accomplished. A second class period will be used to enable each student to tour the Constantine village cemetery. At the cemetery, the students will get an overall sense of the history of the village and the surrounding area, and each student will select one person as the focus person for his or her research. The teacher will make available some additional class time as the project progresses for the students to ask questions and share some of their more interesting discoveries.

Resources Needed

Students will have the use of a number of available local primary resources. Initially, the high school learning resources center will make available to all students common community resource material as well as several specific resource books. Local newspapers will be contacted to make newspaper libraries available to the students. The Constantine village library will make available a unique file of local obituaries that will assist students in finding information on the person selected for their research and also assist in locating living family members. Students will be encouraged to locate and interview living relatives on the subject of their research to obtain firsthand information about the person and his or her life in Constantine.

Procedure

This project is meant to encompass an entire semester starting with two specific lessons. The first lesson will last one period and will consist of an orientation session conducted by the teacher. The teacher will outline the purpose of the lesson and the goals to be accomplished. Each step of the project will be explained and all questions will be answered. Careful instruction will be given by the teacher for the procedure to be followed during the visit to the village cemetery. Particular emphasis will be placed on the importance of a respectful visit, and students will learn the specific information that each will need to begin the project. The second lesson will be a one class period visit to the cemetery, with the teacher assisting students in understanding how to read certain headstones. Each student will pick at least one person buried in the cemetery as the focus of his or her investigation. During the remainder of the semester, students will be provided with opportunities to visit the high school learning resources center where a list of school and community resources will be available on a special cart. This cart will contain a number of unique printed resources, including primary resources, that may assist students in the search for their "persons" and the times in which the persons lived. During the semester, the teacher will schedule regular meetings with individual students to monitor progress and provide assistance as needed. At the end of the semester, each student will provide a research paper reporting the results of his or her investigation. The teacher will evaluate the paper and provide individual feedback to all students.

Assessment

After the visit to the Constantine village cemetery, the teacher will meet with each student to ensure that he or she has some identifying data sufficient to begin an investigation. During the course of the project, the teacher will meet with each student to monitor progress. At the conclusion of the project, each student is required to submit a research paper, typewritten, three to five pages in length. This paper is to be written in an established format taught by the English department. During the time of this project, the English department will be teaching research paper preparation, so the English and American history assignments are meant to be complementary. This paper will be graded, and each student will be given individual feedback in a meeting with the teacher. See the appendix for the research paper-scoring rubric.

Expanded Rationale

The course associated with this lesson plan is U.S. history. Speaking with students at the beginning of the semester determined that students were interested in the history of the United States, but had little knowledge or interest in local history as it relates to certain periods of U. S. history. The lesson will enable students to see that history in our village is a part of greater U.S. history and also the role that our community played in the development of our nation. It will enable students and local citizens to interact and share knowledge about the history of our village.

Extension and Enrichment

This lesson could be followed up by a Constantine village history week. During the week, community members and students could come together to share information about the history of our area. Projects relating to Constantine history could be initiated. Examples of Constantine history projects could include a walking tour of historic homes in our village, featuring several homes that still contain underground hiding places for escaped slaves traveling to Canada via the Underground Railroad, and a play that could tell of the life of Governor Barry of Michigan, a native of Constantine. Constantine was one of the early capitals of Michigan. Contact could be made with local members of Civil War reenactment units to provide a program on several famous Michigan Civil War Regiments from the Constantine/St. Joseph County area.

Resources

Donnelly, William. "Constantine." *Rural America: A Social and Educational History of Ten Communities*. Cambridge, Mass.: ABT Associates Inc., 1975.

Dunbar, Willis F. *Michigan*. Grand Rapids, Mich.: William B. Eerdmans Publishing Co., 1965.

From a Meek Beginning—Village of Constantine. Constantine, Mich., 1978. Philadelphia, Penn.: L.H. Everts & Co., 1877.

Appendix

Name _____

Assignment _____

Date _____

Evaluation Rubric (scoring sheet)

5   Error free; excellent effort

4   Minor errors; accurate; good effort

3   Several errors or inaccuracies; needs more effort

2   Far too many errors or inaccuracies; extremely weak

1   Effort barely evident

Content

1. _____   Title—clear and creative

2. _____   Introductory paragraph—good attention getter; sentences move smoothly from first to last

3. _____   Thesis statement clearly stated

4. _____   Content, sequence are clear in introductory paragraph

5. _____   Content accurately follows outline

6. _____   Paragraph 2—topic sentence

7. _____   Supporting details, examples from research

8. _____   Paragraph 3—topic sentence

9. _____   Supporting details, examples from research

10. _____   Paragraph 4—topic sentence

11. _____   Supporting details, examples from research

12. _____   Additional paragraphs—see above

13. _____   Conclusion—summary; contains no new information

14. _____   "Sources" page contains all sources

15. _____   Grade level sentences; they vary in structure and length

16. _____   Sentences—no fragments, comma splices, or run-ons

17. _____   Punctuation and capitalization

18. _____   Usage/Spelling

19. _____   Correct format followed

20. _____   "Sources" page is alphabetized, follows guidelines

_____   Your score

100 Total points possible

Comments

6 Unions and Collective Bargaining

Mike Koren, Maple Dale School, Maple Dale—Indian Hill School District, Milwaukee, Wisconsin

Grade Level/Subject: Sixth Grade—World History/Economics

NCSS Thematic Strands:

Ⓥ PRODUCTION, DISTRIBUTION, AND CONSUMPTION

g. explain and demonstrate the role of money in everyday life (Early Grades);

f. explain and illustrate how values and beliefs influence different economic decisions (Middle Grades);

i. use economic concepts to help explain historical and current developments and issues in local, national, or global contexts (Middle Grades); and

j. use economic reasoning to compare different proposals for dealing with a contemporary social issue such as unemployment, acid rain, or high-quality education (Middle Grades).

Key Features of Powerful Teaching and Learning

Meaningful—students explore in depth the actions of unions, particularly collective bargaining, a negotiation process the components of which have real life applications;

Value-based—in the simulated negotiating process, students deal with choices that reflect their own attitudes, beliefs, and values. The negotiation process involves opposing points of view and well-supported positions;

Challenging—to reach a fair settlement of the contract, students need to consider many viewpoints and the impact of their decisions. Students also work cooperatively to settle differences; and

Active—students experience the negotiation process through the simulated contract activity. They are actively involved in decision making as ideas and proposals are shared within the process of reaching a new and fair contract. The negotiation process is an authentic activity with real-life applications.

Purpose/Rationale/Introduction

This lesson is taught after the students have studied the Industrial Revolution and its effects on workers. As more and more people went to work in factories during the Industrial Revolution, the working conditions and environment for workers deteriorated. Therefore, workers found it necessary to act collectively to improve their working conditions. This led to the rise of unions to help the workers. The lesson has students explore the goals most unions have and activities unions may conduct to achieve their goals, and engages students in a simulation about the process of negotiating a new contract.

Objectives (Students will):

a. explain the purposes and activities of unions;

b. express views related to provisions of a negotiated collective bargaining agreement; and

c. demonstrate how the process of collective bargaining works.

Time Allotment: two days

Resources Needed
Forms: Problem Statement, Existing Contract at the Stu Dent School Supplies Corporation, and New Contract Provisions (see appendix)

Procedure
1. Ask the students if any of their family members belong to a union. If the students answer yes, ask which unions their family member(s) has/have joined. Ask students what unions are and what they do. Ask students to define the term union. One definition is the following: An organization of workers that seeks to secure good wages and working conditions, to protect workers' rights, and to safeguard workers' jobs. (Feel free to give examples of each of the components of the definition.) Goals of unions include getting good wages, having decent working hours, maintaining and improving working conditions, and saving and protecting jobs.

2. Review with students why unions formed. As factories grew in the United States, it became very hard for workers to earn a decent wage. With immigrants coming into the United States, there was an oversupply of workers. As more people worked in factories and the size of factories grew, the relationship between workers and employer became distant at best, and non-existent at worst. To improve their lot, the workers had to act as a group, not individually. Otherwise, little pressure could be brought upon the employer to make changes.

3. Present the term *contract*. A contract is a legal document between the union (workers) and the company. This document covers all conditions of employment.

4. Ask students to indicate what unions can do to bring pressure upon the employer or company to get a new contract. (Listed below from least to most severe—you may need to share with students if they can't come up with any ideas.)

   a. Informational picketing—workers march with signs outside the place of employment. This is usually done peacefully.

   b. Withdrawal of special services—workers do their jobs but no more. Participation in company-sponsored extracurricular or community activities stops. These may include community fund-raisers, picnics, or recreational activities.

   c. Slowdown—workers go to work but work at slower than normal rates.

   d. Boycott—the union urges its members and the community not to buy the products produced by the firm.

   e. Strike—workers don't come to work if no new contract agreement is reached. Indicate to students that a strike situation is often a very difficult situation for the workers. Workers don't get paid during a strike, and, quite possibly, workers may lose their jobs. They may also not recover the lost wages if the strike is a long one.

5. Present the term collective bargaining. The union (workers) and the company sit down to try to reach a new contractual agreement. Collective bargaining may take several months or longer, or it may be a relatively short process. Give examples of this. One would be the major

league baseball negotiations that began in 1994, which took years to settle. Teachers could point out that the government sometimes gets involved in settling or temporarily ending a strike. The American Airlines pilot strike is an example of this situation. When the old contract expires, both sides may agree to extend the old one until a new agreement is reached.

6. Activity

    a.   Hand out the existing contract for the Stu Dent School Supplies Corporation and discuss its parts. Explain each part in detail. For example, discuss the concept of a percentage pay increase for all workers versus a flat cent (e.g., twenty-five cents an hour) increase for all workers. Also, discuss the concept of insurance, sick days, and other provisions that students may not understand.

    b.   Hand out the Problem Statement page and discuss it with students.

    c.   Divide students into groups of four. Each group represents one company, unrelated to any other groups in the classroom. Two students will represent management of the group, while the other two students will represent the labor union.

    d.   Before starting to negotiate, the two management representatives and the two union representatives from each group will meet separately to discuss possible changes in the contract. When both sides are ready, they will go face-to-face to negotiate. Twenty to twenty-five minutes should be enough time. (Groups that can't reach agreement may need to come at lunch or before/after school to finish the negotiations. This will help students realize that negotiations that don't go smoothly may cause inconvenience in the lives of those who are negotiating.)

    e.   Students will write down terms of the new agreement as they negotiate on the "New Contract Provisions" page. Students should be very specific and detailed when writing each detail on the page. The final contract will be signed by the management and labor representatives.

    f.   After all groups have finished, students will share their thoughts about the process and what they accomplished (or didn't accomplish) in their group. Be sure to discuss what factors allowed the groups to operate smoothly or to experience difficulties. Feel free to offer your opinion of the new contract each group developed. Discuss the strengths and weaknesses of the new document negotiated.

7. Review the main concepts of the lesson.

Assessment

Discussing the process with the students after completion of the activity will help the teacher determine if objectives have been achieved. Also, the finalized contract for each group will help in assessing the students' application of learnings.

Appendix

Problem Statement

The Stu Dent School Supply Corporation, in Glendale, Wisconsin, is a company that produces supplies for schools. This company has about fifty-five employees, most of whom work full time. The workers are represented by a union that has a very good working relationship with the company. There have been no strikes with the company at any time in its history. The union and the company usually agree to and sign contracts lasting two years.

The present contract with the company expires today. The union and the company have been negotiating for the past two months. Within the past few years, the company has had a profit of 10.8%. However, the inflation rate during the same period was 5.4%. While the inflation rate currently shows no signs of changing, there is the possibility this may not be true in the future. The company is also very concerned about the increasing cost of health insurance, which is rising about 10% a year. Currently, the company pays about $7,500 per year for each worker who has a family health insurance plan, and about $3,750 per year for each worker who has a single health insurance plan. Time for a settlement before the contract expires is running out very quickly.

The management of this company wants to continue its good relationship with the union. However, the goal of management is to maximize profits for the company and its shareholders. This is its main objective.

The union negotiators must consider what would happen if the rate of inflation changed. A rise in the inflation rate during the duration of the new contract could mean the workers would earn less money in real dollar terms.

Handout 1

Existing Contract at the Stu Dent School Supplies Corporation

Pay Scale: $5.50 to $7.75 an hour depending on length of service

0-1 year	$5.50
1-3 years	$6.00
4-5 years	$6.50
6-8 years	$7.00
9-12 years	$7.40
Over 13 years	$7.75

Overtime Provisions: Time and a half for working over 40 hours a week. Double time will be paid on Sundays and holidays.

Paid Holiday: New Year's Day, Good Friday, Memorial Day, July 4th, Labor Day, Thanksgiving Day, and the Friday after it, Christmas Eve and Day (December 24 and 25), New Year's Eve (December 31).

Note: All workers will be given three personal days off from work with pay. (This will allow other religious groups to celebrate their holidays with pay.)

Vacation: Zero to six weeks depending on length of service.

0-1 year:	no vacation
1-3 years:	1 week
4-6 years:	2 weeks
7-9 years:	3 weeks
10-12 years:	4 weeks
13-17 years:	5 weeks
Over 18 years:	6 weeks

Insurance: The company will pay for health, dental, and vision insurance.

Sick Days: Ten days per year. Unused sick days may be accumulated up to 150 days.

Length of Current Contract: 2 years

New Contract Provisions at the Stu Dent School Supplies Corporation

Pay Scale:

Overtime Provisions:

Hours per Week and the Hours of the Workday:

Paid Holidays:

Vacation:

Insurance:

Sick Days:

Length of Contract (in years):

The Management and Union of the Stu Dent School Supplies Corporation Agree to the Above Written Terms of This Contract.

Management Signatures

_____

_____

Union Signatures

_____

_____

Date:_____

Transportation on the Move

Paula Ann Mulford, Fisher Model Elementary School, Richmond Public Schools, Richmond, Virginia

Grade Level/Subject: First Grade—Social Studies

NCSS Thematic Strands:

❶ CULTURE (Early Grades)

b. give examples of how experiences may be interpreted differently by people from diverse cultural perspectives and frames of reference.

❷ TIME, CONTINUITY, AND CHANGE (Early Grades)

b. demonstrate an ability to use correct vocabulary associated with time such as past, present, future, and long ago; read and construct simple timelines; identify examples of change; and recognize examples of cause and effect relationships; and

c. compare and contrast different stories or accounts about past events, people, places, or situations, identifying how they contribute to our understanding of the past.

❸ PEOPLE, PLACES, AND ENVIRONMENTS (Early Grades)

h. examine the interactions of human beings and their physical environment...

Key Features of Powerful Teaching and Learning

Meaningful—students are involved in a variety of learning activities related to different forms of transportation, many of which have life application in the present day;

Integrative—this lesson was designed to enable students to think critically about ways people might travel then and now;

Challenging—students must be creative in their use of different media to represent their form of transportation. Students will draw, color, and cut large models out of tag board to illustrate their form of transportation; and

Active—students are critically and creatively thinking as they actively construct a form of transportation of their choice and make connections with other modes of transportation.

Purpose/Rationale/Introduction

Movement and transportation are an integral part of our history. First grade students, over a one week period, will compare transportation forms and their changes from the past to present. Movement—going from one place to another—is a basic theme of geography. Students will construct models and timelines of transportation as culminating activities.

Objectives (Students will):

a. describe the purpose of transportation in society;

b. list different ways people move from place to place;

c. differentiate land, water, and air transportation;

d. identify similarities and differences of various modes of transportation in the past and present;

e. draw, color, and cut out picture models of transportation;

f. create a simple timeline using past and present felt-back pictures;

g. construct large models of transportation out of cardboard boxes; and

h. role-play driving forms of transportation on land, on water, and in the air.

Time Allotment: one week with two, thirty-minute sessions each day—one session in the morning with the second in the afternoon

Resources Needed

1. photographs of different forms of transportation;

2. drawing and coloring materials;

3. felt material;

4. painting materials; and

5. cardboard boxes.

Procedure

Begin the lesson by sharing with students the following pictures of land transportation: horse, covered wagon, model-T car, modern car, and metro subway car. A class discussion about each picture would include the following: What is this picture of? Where is this picture located?

Introduce the words *transportation* and *movement* to the students. Is this a picture of transportation? How do you know? How is it moving?

Introduce the words *past* and *present*. Show one felt card with the word *past* on it. Place it on a large flannel board in front of the class. Place a felt line on the flannel board in a horizontal position under the word *past*.

Introduce and explain the word *timeline* to the students. Show another card with the word *present* on it and place it on the flannel board. Explain the meaning of "present" to the students. Compare the difference of past and present transportation with the students.

The afternoon session will begin with the students together on the carpet. The students will review the material from the morning session. Call on students to come up to place felt words and the felt timeline on the flannel board. Now divide the students into small cooperative groups. Give out small flannel boards and felt picture cards of differing forms of land transportation and felt timelines to each group. Have the children place the cards on the flannel board according to past or present time. There should be twenty different felt-back picture cards of land transportation for the children to display and explain their creations to the entire class. This is a cooperative group effort and everyone has a part.

The children in the cooperative groups select one form of transportation and, working together, they create one picture as a model for a future means of transportation. Each group shares its form of transportation with the entire class. The class is shown many sizes, shapes, and colors of cardboard boxes. Ask the following questions: Could this be turned into a form of transportation that goes on land? What about the water, or sky? Could this become a form of past transportation? How? Could this be turned into a present day form of transportation? How? The teacher now displays the many boxes in an open floor area. The students take their picture model from their group work and select the boxes needed to construct their form of transportation. The glue, paper, paints, and brushes needed are placed in each cooperative group work area, and the children in their groups start building their form of transportation.

Both morning and afternoon sessions are building sessions. As the teacher walks around to the groups, discussions should be initiated about the transportation forms: Where might this move from? Where might it be going? Could it be carrying something? What might it be?, etc.

The transportation creations are presented to the entire class. Students will describe where their form of transportation can be used. Students will explain if it was used in the past or the present time. Invite children to take turns pantomiming an imaginary trip with their box-form of transportation. Using the rope for the floor timeline, place the models of the group transportation on the timeline. Each group can select one child to lay down its picture on the floor. Next, the students can get their individual pictures to lay down on the timeline under either past or present labels.

Assessment
Students will describe where their form of transportation can be used: land, water, or sky. Students will explain if it was used in the past or is used in the present. The presentations are rated on a scale of 1 to 5. To receive a 5, the group must explain in significant detail the answers to the two key questions: How would you describe your form of transportation? and Explain how it was used in the past or present.

Extensions
Link technology to the world of transportation by using the computer. Travel the Internet and visit websites on different types of past and present transportation forms. Download and print transportation pictures to create a transportation book. On the computer, share with the class the video of Orville and Wilbur Wright's first flight. Compare and contrast it with a video of Neil Armstrong taking his first steps on the moon.

Teacher Resource List
Lee Bennett Hopkins. *I've Got A Rocket*. New York: Harcourt Brace and Company, 1977.
Alvin Tresselt. *Wake Up, City!* New York: Lothrop, Lee and Shepard, 1990.

Children's Resource List
Barbara Cooney. *Island Boy*. New York: Viking, 1988.
Peter Sis. *Follow the Dream*. New York: Knopf, 1991.

Glidden's Patent Application for Barbed Wire

Emily Ray, Richmond, Virginia and Wynell Schamel, Education Branch, National Archives and Records Administration, Washington, D.C.

Grade Level/Subject: Middle School and High School—U.S. History

NCSS Thematic Strands:

Ⓥ SCIENCE, TECHNOLOGY, AND SOCIETY

a.   identify and describe both current and historical examples of the interaction and interdependence of science, technology, and society in a variety of cultural settings; (High School)

b.   make judgments about how science and technology have transformed the physical world and human society and our understanding of time, space, place and human-environment interactions; (High School)

b.   show through specific examples how science and technology have changed people's perceptions of the social and natural world, such as in their relationship to the land, animal life, family life and economic needs, wants and security; (Middle Grades)

c.   explain the need for laws and policies to govern scientific and technological applications,…. (Middle Grades)

Ⓘ TIME, CONTINUITY, AND CHANGE

d.   systematically employ processes of critical historical inquiry to reconstruct and reinterpret the past, such as using a variety of sources and checking their credibility,…. (High School)

e.   investigate, interpret and analyze multiple historical and contemporary viewpoints within and across cultures related to important events, recurrent dilemmas and persistent issues, while employing empathy, skepticism and critical judgement; (High School)

c.   identify and use processes important to reconstructing and reinterpreting the past, such as using a variety of sources, providing, validating, and weighing evidence for claims, checking credibility of sources, and searching for causality; (Middle Grades)

f.   use knowledge of facts and concepts drawn from history, along with methods of historical inquiry, to inform decision-making about and action-taking on public issues. (Middle Grades)

Purpose/Rationale/Introduction

Life in the American West was reshaped by a series of patents for a simple tool that helped ranchers tame the land: barbed wire. Nine patents for improvements to wire fencing were granted by the U.S. Patent Office to American inventors, beginning with Michael Kelly in November 1868 and ending with Joseph Glidden in November 1874. Barbed wire not only simplified the work of the rancher and farmer, but it significantly affected political, social, and economic practices throughout the region. The swift emergence of this highly effective tool as

* This article was reprinted from Social Education *61, 1 (January 1997): 53-56.*

the favored fencing method influenced life in the region as dramatically as the rifle, six-shooter, telegraph, windmill, and locomotive.

Barbed wire was extensively adopted because it proved ideal for western conditions. Vast and undefined prairies and plains yielded to range management, farming, and ultimately widespread settlement. As the use of barbed wire increased, wide open spaces became less wide, less open, and less spacious, and the days of the free roaming cowboy were numbered. Today, cowboy ballads remain as nostalgic reminders of life before barbed wire became an accepted symbol of control, transforming space to place and giving new meaning to private property. Before the invention of barbed wire, the lack of effective fencing limited the range of farming and ranching practices, and with it, the number of people who could settle in an area. Wooden fences were costly and difficult to acquire on the prairie and plains, where few trees grew. Lumber was in such short supply in the region that farmers were forced to build houses of sod. Likewise, rocks for stone walls—commonly found in New England—were scarce on the plains. Shrubs and hedges, early substitutes for wood and rock fencing materials, took too long to grow to become of much use in the rapidly expanding West. Barbed wire was cheaper, easier, and quicker to use than any of these other alternatives.

Without fencing, livestock grazed freely, competing for fodder and water. Where working farms existed, most property was unfenced and open to foraging cattle and sheep. Once a year, cattle owners, unhindered by fenced property lines, led their herds on long cattle drives, eventually arriving at slaughter houses located near urban railheads for shipping convenience. The appearance of barbed wire meant the end of both the open range and the freedom of rancher and cowboy, an event lamented in the Cole Porter song "Don't Fence Me In."

Wire fences used before the invention of the barb consisted of only one strand of wire, which was constantly broken by the weight of cattle pressing against it. Michael Kelly made a significant improvement to wire fencing with an invention that "twisted two wires together to form a cable for barbs—the first of its kind in America," according to Henry D. and Frances T. McCallum, the authors of *The Wire That Fenced the West*. Known as the "thorny fence," Kelly's double-strand design made the fence stronger, and the painful barbs taught cattle to keep their distance.

Predictably, other inventors sought to improve upon Kelly's designs; among them was Joseph Glidden, a farmer from De Kalb, Illinois. In 1873 and 1874, patents were issued for various designs to strengthen Kelly's invention, but the recognized winner in this series of improvements was Glidden's simple wire barb locked onto a double-strand wire. Glidden's invention made barbed wire more effective not only because he described a method for locking the barbs in place, but also because he developed the machinery to mass-produce the wire. His invention also survived court challenges from other inventors. Glidden's patent, prevailing in both litigation and sales, was soon known as "the winner." Today it remains the most familiar style of barbed wire.

The widespread use of barbed wire changed life on the Great Plains dramatically and permanently. Land and water once open to all were fenced off by ranchers and homesteaders with predictable results. Cattlemen, increasingly cut off from what they regarded as common-use resources in such territories as Texas, New Mexico, Colorado, and Wyoming, first filed land-use petitions and then waged fierce range wars against the property-owning farmers. Gradually, there was a discernible shift in who controlled the land and thus wielded the superior power.

Living patterns were radically altered for nomadic Native Americans as well. Further squeezed from lands they had always used, they began calling barbed wire "the Devil's rope." Fenced-off land meant that more and more cattle herders—regardless of race—were dependent on the dwindling public lands, which rapidly became overgrazed. The harsh winter of 1886, culminating in a big January 1887 blizzard, wreaked further havoc on the cattle market: losses totalled more than $20 million in Wyoming alone. In effect, large-scale, open range cattle enterprises disappeared.

While barbed wire symbolized the range wars and the end of widespread open grazing land for livestock in the American West, it also became a widely used commodity elsewhere, especially for land warfare. In early European history, pointed spears or palisades circumferentially surrounded many castles for protection. Barbed wire rapidly replaced these and other devices used to protect people and property from unwanted intrusion. Military usage of barbed wire formally dates to 1888, when British military manuals first encouraged its use.

During the Spanish American War, Teddy Roosevelt's Rough Riders chose to defend their camps with the help of barbed wire. In turn-of-the-century South Africa, five-strand fences were linked to blockhouses sheltering British troops from the encroachment of Boer commandos. During World War I, barbed wire was used as a military weapon. It was a formidable barrier along the front stretching from Switzerland to the English Channel. Even now, it is widely used to protect and safeguard military installations and to establish territorial boundaries.

Barbed wire has emerged as a commonly recognized instrument for prisoner confinement, and the image of a corpse caught on the wires of a concentration camp fence has become the emblem/embodiment of war's ravages. Today barbed wire is often part of the containment wall of prisons all over the world.

Other less emotionally charged uses of barbed wire fencing exist in industry. Used on construction sites, storage sites, and warehouses, barbed wire protects supplies and persons and keeps out unwanted intruders. In any event, it has proved both highly useful and highly significant in altering traditional practices during both war and peace.

Glidden's patent, No. 157124, was issued November 24, 1874. The patent application and related papers are found in the Records of the Patent and Trademark Office, Record Group 241, at the National Archives and Records Administration.

Procedure

1. Document Analysis

Divide students into pairs, and ask them to take turns "free-associating" or describing aloud any words or images they associate with barbed wire. Then ask them to discuss ways in which this object has become a symbol of the romance of the old West, of war and destruction, and of confinement.

Project a transparency of the patent drawing on an overhead projector, read the written description aloud, and then ask the students the following questions: For whom was the drawing intended? Why was it created? What is the inventor actually seeking to patent? What are the strengths of the invention? How well does the written description depict the physical design and intended use? What aspects of the description need enhancement?

Ask students to consider what skills were required for the inventor to design these improvements to wire, and what skills were required to manufacture, market, and sell the product.

Ask the students to connect these skills to professions and technical fields, and list them on the chalkboard. As an optional followup, ask some students to create advertisements for barbed wire. Help them locate a reproduction copy of a 19th-century Sears Roebuck catalog. Project copies of student designs and pages from the catalog advertising barbed wire on an overhead projector, and ask the class to compare the two sets of designs.

2. Writing and Defining a Position

Divide the class into four groups, and instruct each group to research and prepare a position on the invention as follows: first group, cowboys or herders; second, farmers; third, Native Americans; and fourth, wire manufacturers. Convene a community meeting to discuss the various viewpoints of each group regarding the safety, privacy, and other issues related to the invention.

3. Comparing Written and Visual Descriptions

Ask students to write a description of an improvement for an object they use regularly in the classroom, such as a pencil sharpener, chalkboard, or desk. Pair the students, and instruct them to take turns reading the description aloud to their partners, who must draw their impressions of what the object looks like. Ask them to assess the accuracy of the results and to explore reasons why the visual and verbal descriptions matched or failed to match. Then discuss with the class why the patent office requires both written and visual descriptions of patent applications.

4. Relating Personal Experiences

Collecting barbed wire is a popular hobby. The Barbed Wire Museum in Canyon, Texas, has over 200 specimens of barbed wire in its collection. Currently, there is an exhibit at the National Building Museum that features barbed wire. Ask your students what their encounters with barbed wire have been. Also ask them how they would account for the continued fascination with barbed wire.

5. Creative Interpretation

Locate the words and a recording of Cole Porter's song "Don't Fence Me In." Ask the class to identify the point of view of the singer as you project the words from a transparency and play the recording. Ask students to translate the images raised by the songwriter into another medium, such as a drawing, pantomime, poem, or dance. Encourage some students to take another viewpoint related to the changes produced by barbed wire, and to express those feelings in an appropriate medium.

6. Further Research Activity

Ask for volunteers to research other inventions or improvements to inventions that significantly influenced the changing landscape of the American West, such as the rifle, six-shooter, telegraph, windmill, and locomotive. Arrange for these students to conduct a panel discussion for the class on the effects of these improvements on life in the West.

UNITED STATES PATENT OFFICE.

JOSEPH F. GLIDDEN, OF DE KALB, ILLINOIS.

IMPROVEMENT IN WIRE FENCES.

Specification forming part of Letters Patent No. **157,124,** dated November 24, 1874; application filed October 27, 1873.

To all whom it may concern:

Be it known that I, JOSEPH F. GLIDDEN, of De Kalb, in the county of De Kalb and State of Illinois, have invented a new and valuable Improvement in Wire Fences; and that the following is a full, clear, and exact description of the construction and operation of the same, reference being had to the accompanying drawings, in which—

Figure 1 represents a side view of a section of fence exhibiting my invention. Fig. 2 is a sectional view, and Fig. 3 is a perspective view, of the same.

This invention has relation to means for preventing cattle from breaking through wire fences; and it consists in combining, with the twisted fence-wires, a short transverse wire, coiled or bent at its central portion about one of the wire strands of the twist, with its free ends projecting in opposite directions, the other wire strand serving to bind the spur-wire firmly to its place, and in position, with its spur ends perpendicular to the direction of the fence-wire, lateral movement, as well as vibration, being prevented. It also consists in the construction and novel arrangement, in connection with such a twisted fence-wire, and its spur-wires, connected and arranged as above described, of a twisting-key or head-piece passing through the fence-post, carrying the ends of the fence-wires, and serving, when the spurs become loose, to tighten the twist of the wires, and thus render them rigid and firm in position.

In the accompanying drawings, the letter B designates the fence-posts, the twisted fence-wire connecting the same being indicated by the letter A. C represents the twisting-key, the shank of which passes through the fence-post, and is provided at its end with an eye, *b*, to which the fence-wire is attached. The outer end of said key is provided with a transverse thumb-piece, *c*, which serves for its manipulation, and at the same time, abutting against the post, forms a shoulder or stop, which prevents the contraction of the wire from drawing the key through its perforation in said post.

The fence-wire is composed at least of two strands, *a* and *z*, which are designed to be twisted together after the spur-wires have been arranged in place.

The letter D indicates the spur-wires. Each of these is formed of a short piece of wire, which is bent at its middle portion, as at E, around one only of the wire strands, this strand being designated by the letter *a*. In forming this middle bend or coil several turns are taken in the wire, so that it will extend along the strand-wire for a distance several times the breadth of its diameter, and thereby form a solid and substantial bearing-head for the spurs, which will effectually prevent them from vibrating laterally or being pushed down by cattle against the fence-wire. Although these spur-wires may be turned at once around the wire strand, it is preferred to form the central bend first, and to then slip them on the wire strand, arranging them at suitable distances apart. The spurs having thus been arranged on one of the wire strands are fixed in position and place by approaching the other wire strands *z* on the side of the bend from which the spurs extend, and then twisting the two strands *a z* together by means of the wire key above mentioned, or otherwise. This operation locks each spur-wire at its allotted place, and prevents it from moving therefrom in either direction. It clamps the bend of the spur-wire upon the wire *a*, thereby holding it against rotary vibration. Finally, the spur ends extending out between the strands on each side, and where the wires are more closely approximated in the twist, form shoulders or stops *s*, which effectually prevent such rotation in either direction.

Should the spurs, from the untwisting of the strands, become loose and easily movable on their bearings, a few turns of the twisting-key will make them firm, besides straightening up the fence-wire.

What I claim as my invention, and desire to secure by Letters Patent, is—

A twisted fence-wire having the transverse spur-wire D bent at its middle portion about one of the wire strands *a* of said fence-wire, and clamped in position and place by the other wire strand *z*, twisted upon its fellow, substantially as specified.

JOSEPH F. GLIDDEN.

Witnesses:
G. L. CHAPIN,
J. H. ELLIOTT.

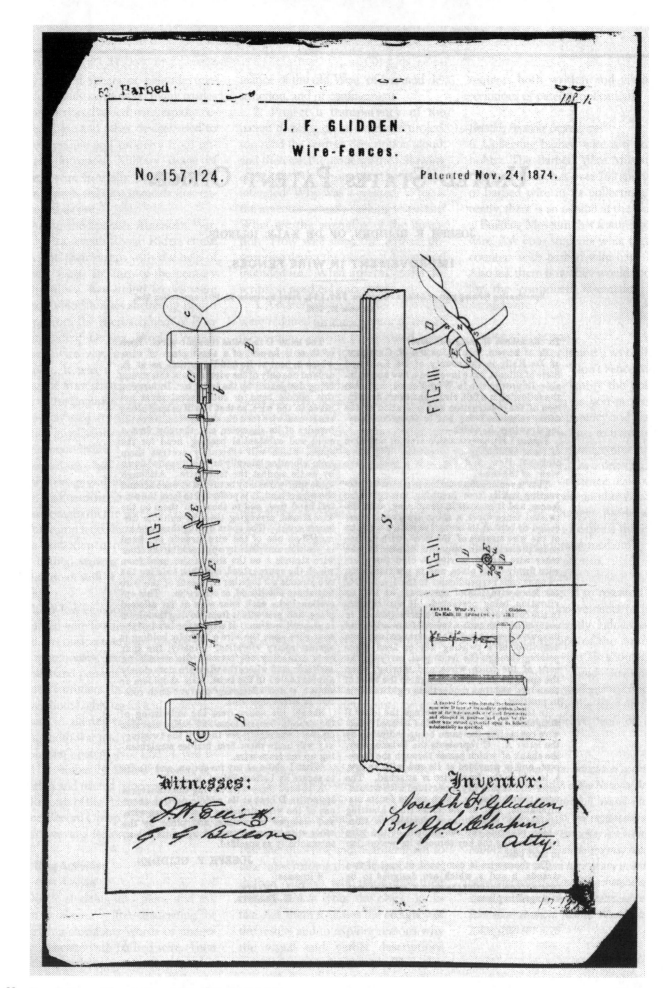

Two Tickets to Freedom

Patricia King Robeson, Maryland Geographic Alliance, UMBC, Baltimore, Maryland

Grade Level/Subject: Fifth Grade—U. S. History

NCSS Thematic Strands:

Ⅲ PEOPLE, PLACES, AND ENVIRONMENTS

c. use appropriate resources, data sources, and geographic tools such as atlases, data bases, grid systems, charts, graphs, and maps to generate, manipulate, and interpret information (Early Grades);

a. elaborate mental maps of locales, regions, and the world that demonstrate understanding of relative location, direction, size, and shape (Middle Grades);

b. create, interpret, use, and distinguish various representations of the earth, such as maps, globes, and photographs (Middle Grades);

d. estimate distance, calculate scale, and distinguish other geographic relationships such as population density and spatial distribution patterns (Middle Grades); and

e. locate and describe varying landforms and geographic features, such as mountains, plateaus, islands, rain forests, deserts, and oceans, and explain their relationships within the ecosystems (Middle Grades).

Ⅶ PRODUCTION, DISTRIBUTION, AND CONSUMPTION

e. describe how we depend upon workers with specialized jobs and the ways in which they contribute to the production and exchange of goods and services (Early Grades);

f. describe the influence of incentives, values, traditions, and habits on economic decisions (Early Grades);

g. explain and demonstrate the role of money in everyday life (Early Grades);

h. describe the relationship of price to supply and demand (Early Grades); and

a. give and explain examples of ways that economic structure choices about how goods and services are to be produced and distributed (Middle Grades);

Key Features of Powerful Teaching and Learning

Meaningful—students engage in in-depth study of a slave couple who escape to freedom. A variety of learning activities involve students in examining and applying geographical and economic concepts and processes. Additionally, students explore meaningful perspectives on the migration of people, civic-mindedness, and people's desire to be free;

Integrated—this lesson includes concepts of economics, geography, history, anthropology, and sociology. Content is also integrated across other language arts areas: literature (non-fiction and poetry) and written and oral communication skills;

Value-based—*Two Tickets to Freedom* is a story to help students develop and understand different perspectives on slavery, injustices caused by the slavery system, the positive role of abolitionists, and the freedoms slaves acquired when escaping;

Challenging—students are challenged to read, comprehend, listen carefully, and respond thoughtfully within ethically based discussions related to the controversial issue of slavery. Students also work in cooperative groups using atlases and maps to investigate routes that slaves used to escape, complete a migration chart based on the story, reflect on the chart, and create a verse to a slave song; and

Active—students engage in the active construction of knowledge through interactive discourse in cooperative groups to complete two performance-based assessments.

Purpose/Rationale/Introduction:

What would it be like to try and escape to freedom, especially if you were a slave and had to travel a great distance? As students read a true story about a fugitive slave couple, they engage in an in-depth study of all aspects of slavery, including its ethical dimensions.

Objectives (Students will):

a.   describe how the Crafts migrated from the South to the North by exchanging goods and services;

b.   describe how the Crafts used various modes of transportation;

c.   explain how the Crafts were dependent on many people;

d.   explain how the physical setting of the land helped and hindered the Crafts' escape;

e.   identify and describe the slavery period of our country and the impact it had on people's lives;

f.   explain how the Crafts worked independently and cooperatively to reach their goals;

g.   use the Drinking Gourd song to examine physical and cultural patterns and ways people used physical features of the land to assist them in gaining freedom; and

h.   construct a map showing the routes traveled by the Crafts on their escape to freedom.

Time Allotment: this book contains ninety-three pages that are divided into nine chapters. This lesson can be completed in three sessions with the students doing some independent reading.

Resources Needed

1.   Florence B. Freedman. *Two Tickets to Freedom*. New York: Scholastic, Inc., 1971;

2.   U.S. map;

3.   outline map of the United States, Canada, and Great Britain to map the Craft's journey (see appendix);

4.   migration chart (see appendix), two copies for each student;

5.   "Follow the Drinking Gourd" song (see appendix); and

6.   student atlases.

Procedure

Setting for the Story

1. Explain to the students that the book they are about to read is a true story about two fugitive slaves, William and Ellen Craft. The story begins early in the morning on Wednesday, December 21, 1848. Ask students to explain how Florence Freedman found information to write this story. After students have made several guesses, turn to the last page in the book and read the information on "Sources" to the students. Discuss how primary source materials were used to obtain factual information for the story.

2. Divide the class into groups of four, and give each group an atlas and an outline map of the United States, Canada, and Great Britain. Instruct them to use the atlas and plan a route that they think, as a group, the Crafts may have traveled from Macon, Georgia, to Halifax, Nova Scotia, Canada. Instruct them to draw the route on their map and to label cities, waterways, mountains, and other landmarks that they think the Crafts would have traveled through or crossed to reach Canada.

3. Instruct the students to think about the date, 1848, and on the back of the map to list the modes of transportation the Crafts may have used on their journey.

4. Explain to the students that this is a chapter book, which will take several days to read. As they read, they will be looking for information to complete the migration chart. After giving students a copy, instruct them to examine it so that they will know what information to look for as they read.

5. Begin to read the book *Two Tickets to Freedom*.

6. Story Discussion Activity

   a. Explain how the Crafts were able to acquire the resources they needed to escape. (Slaves were not allowed to trade with Whites unless they had permission from their master, and many storekeepers were not willing to sell articles to slaves; but William was able to find some sympathetic men who would trade and sell items to him. Ellen made trousers. William saved money that his master had allowed him to earn by making cabinets.)

   b. Explain how the Crafts used the money and skills (human resources) they accumulated to make their dream come true. (The Crafts used the money they saved to buy tickets to travel on trains, boats, and carriages. They also used some of the money to pay for shelter and clothing. They used their skills as a seamstress and a cabinetmaker to earn more money.)

   c. Compare and contrast how the Crafts' plan of escape was different from that of other slaves who escaped. (Ellen, being of very light skin, traveled as a White male with her disguise, and William traveled as her slave. They traveled the way Whites would during the time of slavery. Other slaves had to use the Underground Railroad and hide in houses and never use public transportation. The Crafts and all slaves had to be very aware of "slave hunters.")

   d. Explain how the physical features of the land helped or hindered the Crafts in their escape. (In those days, people traveled long distances by train, boat, or horse and carriage. To take the shortest routes often meant traveling by water. The Crafts traveled across and on many rivers. They traveled along the flat land of the East

Coast. Every time the Crafts came to a city, they had to change to trains, boats, or carriages. Their chances of getting caught were much greater because people were always looking for runaway slaves.)

e. Explain how slaves who used the Underground Railroad depended on human-made and natural/physical features of the land to plan their journey. (Slaves on the Underground Railroad used ponds, streams, trees, fields, houses, etc., to plan their escape route. These features were used as markers to guide the slave. They could hide in forests and in barns and houses.)

f. Explain how the Crafts' standard of living changed from the time they were slaves to when they lived as free persons in England. (In slavery, the Crafts lived in fear of being separated. They were not allowed to have a religious or civil wedding ceremony and were never taught to read or write. William was allowed to keep a little of the money he earned as a cabinetmaker. William taught himself to read and write, and, in England, he became a novelist and playwright and was an eloquent public speaker. He used his talents to promote world peace and the abolition of slavery. Ellen often went with William, and they met many prominent people. In England, William had a good job, and together they were able to have a family and raised four sons and one daughter.)

g. Explain how the Crafts' standard of living changed again when they returned to Georgia. (The Crafts never forgot their roots. They knew that former slaves could not read or write and still lived in poverty. The Crafts decided to use the money they had earned in England to move back to Georgia. They bought a plantation and built a school on their land. They went from having a savings account to having a mortgage of $2,500 in order to provide services for others.)

7. Conclusion/Closure. Give each student a second copy of the outline map of the United States, Canada, and New England. Instruct them to use their migration charts to map the route the Crafts traveled from slavery all the way to England. Allow students to use atlases and instruct them to include map elements: compass rose, key, title, and legend. Instruct them to look at the first map they used to plan the course of travel and compare it to the map they completed after reading the book. Ask students to explain their two maps.

Assessment
Migration Chart
Tell the students to design a stamp for the Crafts. They are to use the information on their migration charts to assist them in recognizing how the Crafts used geography and economics to help them accomplish their goals. When they have designed their stamps, instruct them to write a letter to the U.S. Post Office to persuade them to choose the stamp they designed. The letter should also include information about the design and facts about the Crafts' life that they listed on their migration chart.

"Follow the Drinking Gourd"
Allow students to work in cooperative groups and give each group copies of "Follow the Drinking Gourd." Explain that this song was often sung by slaves escaping to freedom on the Underground Railroad. Because Ellen and William did not use the Underground Railroad, their song would have been different from this one. Instruct the students to write at least one verse of a song that the Crafts might have sung as a result of their journey to freedom. Students may use names of cities, rivers, landmarks, people, etc. Have students share their verse with others.

Name: Answer Key   Date:

Two Tickets to Freedom Migration Chart

Starting Point	Stopping Point	Transportation	Dates	Services Received or Rendered
Macon, GA	Savannah, GA	Train, Horse-drawn Omnibus	December 21, 1848	Bought tickets to escape.
Savannah, GA	Charleston, SC	Steamer, Horse and Carriage		Served dinner in hotel. Bought tickets at Custom House.
Charleston, SC	Wilmington, NC	Steamer		
Wilmington, NC	Richmond, VA	Train		
Richmond, VA	Fredericksburg, VA	Train		
Fredericksburg, VA	Washington, D.C.	Steamer, Horse and Carriage		
Washington, D.C.	Baltimore, MD	Train	December 24, 1848	Conductor allowed Crafts to board the train.
Baltimore, MD	Havre de Grace, MD	Ferryboat, Boat		Conductor found William for Ellen.
Havre de Grace, MD	Philadelphia, PA	Train, Horse and Carriage	December 25, 1848	Boardinghouse owner helped them find shelter.
Philadelphia, PA	Ivens' Farm	Steamer		Ivens sheltered Crafts and taught them to read and write.
Ivens' Farm	Boston, MA	Train	1849	William worked as a cabinet maker and Ellen as a seamstress. Mrs. Loring sheltered Crafts. Theodore Parker married the Crafts in a free state.
Boston, MA	Portland, ME	Train		Mr. May accompanied Crafts to ensure their safety. Mr. Oliver provided shelter.
Portland, ME	St. Johns, New Brunswick, Canada	Steamer		
St. Johns, New Brunswick, Canada	Windsor, Nova Scotia, Canada	Steamer		
Windsor, Nova Scotia, Canada	Halifax, Nova Scotia, Canada	Train and walked last 7 miles		
Halifax, Nova Scotia, Canada	Liverpool, England	Ship, *Cambria*	Two years after their escape from Georgia	Rev. Mr. Canady and Rev. Mr. Bishop provided shelter for the Crafts.
Liverpool, England	Bryan County, Georgia			Established a school on their plantation

Name: Date:

Two Tickets to Freedom Migration Chart

Starting Point	Stopping Point	Transportation	Dates	Services Received or Rendered

Follow the Drinking Gourd

Follow the drinking gourd,

Follow the drinking gourd,

For the old man is waiting

for to carry you to freedom

If you follow the drinking gourd.

When the sun comes back

and the first quail calls,

Follow the drinking gourd,

For the old man is waiting

for to carry you to freedom

If you follow the drinking gourd.

The riverbank will make a very good road,

The dead trees show you the way,

Left foot, peg foot traveling on,

Following the drinking gourd.

The river ends between two hills,

Follow the drinking gourd.

There's another tree on the other side,

Follow the drinking gourd.

Where the great big river meets the little river,

Follow the drinking gourd.

The old man is waiting for

to carry you to freedom,

If you follow the drinking gourd.

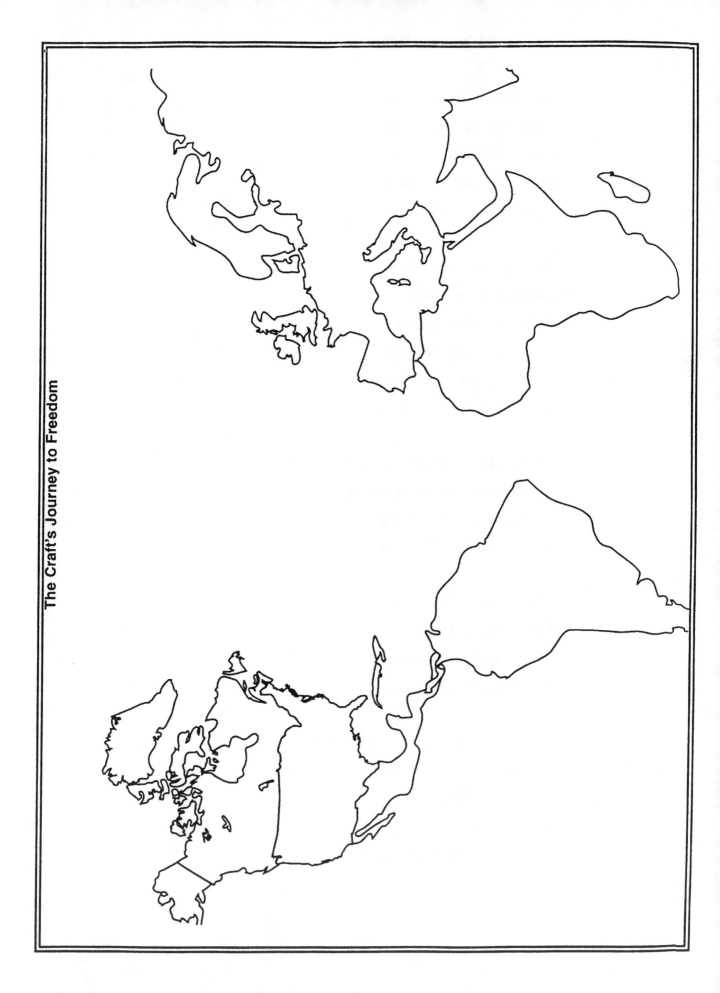

10 Prejudice and Values

Walter F. Urbanek, Dunnellon, Florida

Grade Level/Subject: Ninth Grade—Global Studies

NCSS Thematic Strands:

II TIME, CONTINUITY, AND CHANGE

b. identify and use key concepts such as chronology, causality, change, conflict, and complexity to explain, analyze, and show connections among patterns of historical change and continuity (Middle Grades); and

e. investigate, interpret, and analyze multiple historical and contemporary viewpoints within and across cultures related to important events, recurring dilemmas, and persistent issues, while employing empathy, skepticism, and critical judgment (High School).

VI POWER, AUTHORITY, AND GOVERNANCE

h. explain and apply concepts such as power, role, status, justice, and influence to the examination of persistent issues and social problems (Middle Grades); and

a. examine persistent issues involving the rights, roles, and status of the individual in relation to the general welfare (High School);

V INDIVIDUALS, GROUPS, AND INSTITUTIONS (High School)

d. identify and analyze examples of tensions between expressions of individuality and efforts used to promote social conformity by groups and institutions.

Key Features of Powerful Teaching and Learning

Meaningful—students explore the concept of prejudice as they perceive it and as nations practiced it during a variety of historical periods;

Integrative—students explore concepts and issues that have historical, geographic, and sociological bases;

Value-based—students examine their own attitudes, beliefs, and dispositions related to discrimination and prejudice. Students further explore the instances of genocide and their reaction to these instances;

Challenging—students engage in an investigation of a national group that has undergone extreme prejudice; and

Active—students engage in a variety of activities involving interactive discourse to help them discover their own beliefs and feelings related to discrimination and prejudice.

Purpose/Rationale/Introduction

How could six million Jews be condemned to death because of their ancestry? How could people turn their backs on 1.5 million innocent Jewish children? How could physically and mentally handicapped persons be victims of a Nazi euthanasia program? There are many answers to these questions; however, the basic cause of the Holocaust was prejudice. Prejudice helped shape the political, social, economic, and religious attitudes toward the Jews.

The Nazis used prejudice to increase anti-Semitism to the point where they were able to initiate their programs of genocide. As a result of this lesson, the students will better understand the Holocaust and the problems related to prejudice that plague the modern world.

Objectives (Students will):

a. recognize the relationship between prejudice and our actions as human beings;

b. evaluate the basic causes of prejudice and its impact on a group;

c. identify relationships between prejudice, stereotyping, scapegoating, discrimination, racism, and genocide;

d. identify how our beliefs shape our attitudes and values;

e. describe their own feelings, beliefs, and values;

f. describe the feelings victims of prejudice experience;

g. evaluate information to better understand prejudice with the goal of combating this social problem; and

h. explain how action is needed to protect democratic institutions and civil rights.

Time Allotment: one block of ninety minutes or two regular class periods

Resources Needed
1. Who Am I? chart and questions (see appendix 1);

2. television commercials; and

3. Minority Groups genocide diagram (see appendix 2).

Procedure
1. To prepare for class, the students will define the following terms:
    prejudice
    stereotyping
    anti-Semitism
    scapegoating
    discrimination
    propaganda
    ethnocentrism
    dehumanization
    genocide
    ghetto
    isolation

2. Next, they are to complete the Who Am I? chart and record their answers and reactions to the questions in their journal (see appendix 1).

3. Class begins with a discussion of the student responses on the Who Am I? chart. The goal is to show that all students are members of numerous groups. A list is compiled and recorded on the board of the most and least common responses. As we discuss the responses, we stress the importance of being accepted into a group, and the impact the group has on our attitudes,

values, and actions. Many times behavior is influenced by emotions felt by a group at a particular moment: joy, anger, sorrow, hostility, or compassion.

4. Next, we turn to a discussion of prejudice. After defining and discussing the homework terms, we complete the student response statements that will be distributed to the class. The purpose of the exercise is to illustrate that all of us have prejudices. The list could be adapted to the ethnicity of a specific community. Possible statements might be the following:

> All Native Americans . . .
> All people on welfare . . .
> All African Americans . . .
> All blondes . . .
> All teachers . . .
> All female athletes . . .
> All wrestlers . . .
> All Ford trucks . . .
> All Hispanics . . .
> All people with AIDS . . .
> All fat people . . .
> All Chevrolet trucks . . .
> All people who use drugs . . .
> All gangs . . .
> All gay people . . .
> All boys who play soccer . . .
> All geeks . . .
> All cheerleaders . . .
> All students who eat school lunch . . .
> All boys who play football . . .
> All class officers . . .

When the assignment is completed, list some of the student responses on the board. Discuss the following questions:

a. Is there a pattern that illustrates prejudice?

b. Where do these feelings and beliefs originate?

c. Should we believe everything we hear, read, or see on television?

d. Why is it wrong to refer to all members of a group as "they?"

Discuss the following statement: "The world we perceive is the world we see through words and images."

5. Hold up a blank sheet of paper, explaining that the paper is like a baby when it is born in regard to prejudice—the paper has no marks on it. The child has no negative feelings toward anyone or anything when he/she enters the world. What conclusion can we draw from this analogy? (That everything we know, feel, and believe is learned.)

6. The students will move to assigned cooperative groups and generate a list of things that a child might hear, see, or experience that would cause him or her to become prejudiced against another person or group. The students will record their answers. The responses will be identified and discussed.

7. When the students have completed this exercise, they are to turn the paper over, and, on the backside, record what people feel who have been victims of prejudice and discrimination. Examples: depression, hostility, low self-esteem, etc. Record the responses.

8. Conduct a brief discussion of propaganda to show how it is used by groups and individuals to shape public opinion by developing and manipulating prejudice. View two commercials that are popular with the students that have been recorded from TV and discuss the following questions:

   a. What was the purpose of the commercials?

   b. What were the commercials attempting to achieve?

   c. Do we believe what we hear, believe, and see?

   d. Are we more likely to believe something if we hear the same thing at home, at school, in church, on TV, and from the government?

Stress the importance of making decisions based on fact rather than emotion. Review how we acquire prejudice and stereotypes toward minorities.

The following are examples of how propaganda shapes public opinion. Although the statements are not true, how would you feel and react if you heard or read similar stories? (Your decision should be based on fact not emotion.) What should you do? (Do basic research to find the truth.)

   a. World War I: when the German soldiers invaded Belgium—they threw babies in the air and caught them on their bayonets, raped nuns in a convent, etc.

   b. Gulf War: when Iraqi soldiers entered hospitals in Kuwait—they murdered the patients.

9. Prejudice, stereotyping, scapegoating, and discrimination may, in extreme cases, lead to genocide of a minority group. The students will select one ethnic group from the list of six printed at the bottom of the Minority Group diagram. They will use the diagram to determine if their group has been a victim of discrimination or genocide (see appendix 2).

10. The students will trace the treatment of their group by consulting a variety of sources and record their findings in their journal. Sources include the Internet, *Readers Guide*, Infotrac—Super TOM, SIRS, Facts on File, and *Cambridge University Encyclopedia*. They will also incorporate the following statement in their journals and respond to it: "Given certain social and political conditions, an unassimilated racial or ethnic group could become victims of genocide."

Assessment
Journal entries, classroom participation, behavior and attitude changes, and several writing assignments for which students respond to specific situations, issues, or problems can be used for assessment.

Resources
Steven Spielberg. *Facing History Ourselves* (a guide to the film "Schindler's List"). Brookline, Mass.: Facing History Ourselves National Foundation, Inc., 1993

Appendix 1

Who Am I? chart

- How do you see yourself?
- Do others see you as a leader or follower?
- Do you conform to the rules or are you a rebel?
- How do society's labels influence the way you see yourself?
- Are you tolerant of others?
- How do you feel about minorities?
- Do you have any prejudices?
- Do you feel individual citizens have any responsibility to protect our democratic institutions?
- What are the ramifications of prejudice, racism, and stereotyping in a society?
- What can you as a citizen do to reduce or eliminate the problems caused by prejudice?
- What is happening in our nation?
- What can we do?

Minority Group Chart

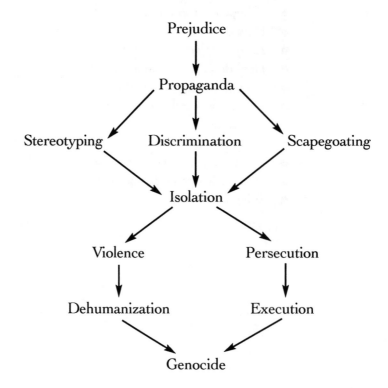

MINORITY GROUP

Prejudice

Propaganda

Stereotyping   Discrimination   Scapegoating

Isolation

Violence   Persecution

Dehumanization   Execution

Genocide

Armenians in Turkey (1915-1916)
Kurds in modern Iraq (1991)
Native Americans (1864-1890)
Cambodians (1975-1979)
Hutu and Tutsi in Africa (1992-1996)
Bosnian Muslims (1992-1995)

Simulation on Ethical and Moral Citizen Responsibilities

Helen O. Willey, Kenmore High School, Akron Public Schools, Akron, Ohio

Grade Level/Subject: High School—American Government

NCSS Thematic Strands:

ⓥ POWER, AUTHORITY, AND GOVERNANCE (High School)
a. examine persistent issues involving the rights, roles, and status in relation to the general welfare; and

b. explain the purpose of government and analyze how its powers are acquired, used, and justified.

ⓧ CIVIC IDEALS AND PRACTICES (High School)
a. explain the origins and interpret the continuing influence of key ideals of the democratic republican form of government, such as individual human dignity, liberty, justice, equality, and the rule of law;

b. identify, analyze, interpret, and evaluate sources and examples of citizens' rights and responsibilities;

c. locate, access, analyze, organize, synthesize, evaluate, and apply information about selected public issues—identifying, describing, and evaluating multiple points of view;

d. practice forms of civic discussion and participation consistent with the ideals of citizens in a democratic republic;

e. analyze and evaluate the influence of various forms of citizen action on public policy;

f. analyze a variety of public policies and issues from the perspective of formal and informal political actors;

g. evaluate the effectiveness of public opinion in influencing and shaping public policy development and decision making;

h. evaluate the degree to which public policies and citizen behaviors reflect or foster the state ideals of a democratic republican form of government;

i. construct a policy statement and an action plan to achieve one or more goals related to an issue of public concern; and

j. participate in activities to strengthen the "common good," based upon careful evaluation of possible options for citizen action.

Key Features of Powerful Teaching and Learning
Meaningful—in this lesson, students are asked to investigate the ethical and moral responsibilities of citizens in a democracy who demonstrate to change public policy. They conduct

an in-depth investigation into the actions of demonstrators at abortion clinics;

Integrative—this lesson was designed to enable students to think critically about both the actions used by citizens and the responsibilities of citizens as they participate in a democracy to change public policy. To accomplish this, students will examine actions of demonstrators in their own communities, the United States, and other democracies over the past decades, and apply skills of planning, decision making, role playing, and discussion as they prepare for, implement, and debrief the action-oriented simulation;

Value-based—the simulation is designed to encourage discussion of a controversial issue, taking into account the opinions of many groups, including pro-life advocates, pro-choice advocates, lawmakers, attorneys, the medical profession, and the media. Students will listen to viewpoints they may oppose and will engage in discussions in a civil manner in considering the ethical and moral responsibilities of citizens in demonstrations intended to change public policy. A culminating assessment is an essay in which students are asked to develop a well-reasoned and supported position on the issue at hand;

Challenging—after investigating the actions of demonstrators and the impact of such demonstrations on laws in the United States, and determining which actions have been traditionally used and which may be considered extreme, the students as a group must design and produce a demonstration that includes citizen actions ranging from those actions traditionally used to those the students consider extreme; and

Active—social simulations, by their very nature, encourage the active involvement of students in body and thought. This simulation is a synthesis of the investigations and critical thinking carried out by the students in considering the ethical and moral responsibilities of citizens as they publicly demonstrate to change public policy on a controversial issue.

Purpose/Rationale/Introduction

In recent years, in attempts to influence public policy, some public demonstrations within democracies (e.g., the United States and Israel) have included extreme actions that may have contributed to a climate of violence and ultimately contributed to the commission of acts of violence. For example, just prior to his assassination, Dr. David Gunn, a doctor who performed abortions in Pensacola, Florida, was portrayed as a murderer on "Wanted" posters and picket signs carried by antiabortion demonstrators demonstrating at the clinic that employed him in Florida. Prime Minister of Israel Yitzhak Rabin was pictured on posters as a Nazi SS officer, traitor, and murderer at an anti-peace-process demonstration prior to his assassination.

Students need to consider the ethical and moral responsibilities of a citizenry within a democracy when demonstrating to change public policy and to assess the need for regulations at public demonstrations to protect the safety of citizens associated with unpopular, but legal, activities.

Objectives (Students will):

a. observe various techniques used by those demonstrating to influence public policy;

b. assess the possible impact and consequences of these techniques used by those demonstrating; and

c. debate the ethical and moral responsibilities of citizens in a democracy to others when demonstrating to change public policy.

Time Allotment: two, forty minute periods

Resources Needed
A variety of materials of sufficient quantity for students to make protest signs.

Procedure
Prior to the first day of the class activity, students are asked to think of groups of demonstrators that they have heard about or studied, and select a group that has engaged in a great range of protest actions, including actions that would be considered by many to cross the line between acceptable and unacceptable forms of protest. Students are told that some of them will commence the activity by simulating a group planning a demonstration, while other members of the class will observe, analyze and discuss the protest. (In this case, the students chose to focus on a group of anti-abortion demonstrators for the simulation described in the lesson plan that follows. Any other group of demonstrators could also be selected, provided that they engage in a broad range of protest actions that trigger important questions about the ethical and moral responsibilities of demonstrators.)

Day One
1. On the day of the simulation, the seats in the classroom are arranged to accommodate the simulation and subsequent discussion. The simulated setting is the living room of a home in which the protesters plan an antiabortion demonstration while the rest of the class observes. Two long tables in the front of the room are needed to accommodate the demonstrators and their visuals. Signs and posters can be displayed on the chalkboard behind the tables as the simulation progresses. Desks in the classroom should be arranged in a semicircle so that all students can easily view the simulation. One student participating in the simulation should be seated in the "living room" before beginning the lesson. The remaining participants will enter when signaled.

2. To begin the lesson, students in the class are told that they are going to witness the planning stages of a public demonstration against abortion. The intent of the demonstration is to change the laws on abortion. Instruct the students to focus on the techniques to be used by the demonstrators and think about the impact of the techniques.

3. The simulation begins with a knock on the door and the entrance of the group into the "home." The group members first discuss blocking the entrance to the clinic and chaining themselves to the door, then walking on to a cemetery carrying crosses and dolls. Next the group focuses on the use of picket signs, which state "Abortion Is Immoral" or depict a doctor who performs the abortions in the clinic, referring to the doctor as a murderer and including his address and phone number. Members of the group discuss taking the license plate numbers of those patients entering the clinic to possibly find out their phone numbers and call their homes. Finally, one member of the group declares that he will use violence to close the clinic and end the abortions. At this point, the simulation ends. (Time for the simulation: fifteen minutes.)

Pass out a discussion sheet immediately at the conclusion of the simulation. The central issue for discussion and four focus questions are on the sheet as follows:
■ Issue: What are the ethical and moral responsibilities of a citizen within a democracy when publicly demonstrating to change public policy?

- Questions to consider:
  1. What actions do you consider appropriate during a public demonstration? Inappropriate?
  2. At what point do actions performed during a demonstration cross an ethical line and become unacceptable?
  3. If an action is legal but ethically questionable and someone is hurt as a result of the action, should there be a consequence to the individual who performed the action?
  4. Is extremism used in accomplishing a moral goal acceptable?
  5. Using the simulation as the basis of the discussion, discuss each of the four questions on the discussion sheet. (Time for the discussion: twenty-five minutes.)

Day Two: Assessment

Assessment

The written assessment is a thirty-minute essay. Students evaluate the simulation and assess the class discussion, noting what they consider to be strengths and weaknesses of each major point of view. In addition, students are asked to present and support an argument in which they support, or oppose, the need to regulate extreme actions taken by citizens who demonstrate at public demonstrations to change public policy.

Oral assessment, ten minutes. Following the written assessment, students are given the opportunity to express their evaluations orally to see if the class can reach a consensus on the need for regulations on the actions of citizens at public demonstrations.

Expanded Rationale

This lesson is a culminating critical thinking activity that was developed in conjunction with a unit on special interest groups. In teaching the unit on special interest groups, students were given the opportunity to form their own special interest groups based on an issue of their choice, and to develop a campaign that included a videotaped commercial, which might best accomplish the outcome the group desired. Several groups completed and presented their campaigns. That gave me the opportunity to observe and select those students whose skills matched the demands of the concluding activity for the unit on special interest groups—the simulation presented in this lesson plan.

12 Uncovering Pompeii: Examining Evidence

Michael M. Yell, Hudson Middle School, Hudson, Wisconsin

Grade Level/Subject: Middle School—World Cultures

NCSS Thematic Strands:

❶ TIME, CONTINUITY, AND CHANGE

a. demonstrate an understanding that different scholars may describe the same event or situation in different ways but must provide reasons or evidence for their views (Middle Grades);

d. identify and use processes important to reconstructing and reinterpreting the past, such as using a variety of sources, providing, validating, and weighing evidence for claims, checking credibility of sources, and searching for causality (Middle Grades); and

c. compare and contrast different stories or accounts about past events, people, places, or situations, identifying how they contribute to our understanding of the past (Early Grades).

Key Features of Powerful Teaching and Learning

Meaningful—students engage in in-depth study of a past civilization using an inquiry process that has life application;

Integrative—students study interdisciplinary science and social science perspectives from the areas of geology, history, and archaeology. Students' papers are evaluated by teachers in history and language arts;

Challenging—the basis for the lesson is the inquiry method, which is initiated by a discrepant event. Students analyze a "problem" in a logical and systematic way as guided by the teacher. Students also interact throughout the lesson and are involved in cooperative group work; and

Active—students are actively involved in the construction of knowledge as a result of the discovery nature of inquiry and through interactive discussions with the teacher and fellow students.

Purpose/Rationale/Introduction

The ancient Roman city of Pompeii continues to fascinate us today. Pompeii was destroyed by the volcano Mt. Vesuvius in AD 79. Ironically, the massive volcanic explosion also preserved Pompeii for the archaeologists and historians of today and of the future. In addition to being a fascinating story, Pompeii provides an archaeological snapshot of a Roman city and the people who lived in it.

In this lesson, students examine, think about, and interact regarding viewpoints of various disciplines—the archaeological, the geologic, and the historical. Throughout this lesson, students are in different groupings to facilitate instruction. Initially, they work in groups of three in order to interact with and discuss the selected materials from the above disciplines. Later in the lesson, students work individually to write a creative yet factual historical essay on "Uncovering Pompeii." The lesson concludes with a class discussion of Pompeii and life in a Roman city.

This lesson uses a strategy called the "interactive presentation" in dealing with this content. This teaching strategy has five distinct phases that blend together to form the whole lesson.[1] The phases are (1) discrepant event inquiry, (2) discussion/presentation, (3) cooperative learning activity, (4) writing for understanding activity, and (5) whole class discussion and review.

Objectives (Students will):

a. experience how the various social science disciplines can be integrated to develop a clear understanding of a historical event; and

b. analyze and synthesize statements in groups and individually from an archaeological, historical, and geologic perspective in developing, and explaining, their understanding of the destruction of Pompeii and life in an ancient Roman city.

Time Allotment: three to four class periods

Resources Needed

1. video—*Rome: The Ultimate Empire,* from the Time-Life video series "Lost Civilizations";[2] and

2. Pompeii information sheets (one of the main sources that I used in developing these information sources is *Pompeii: The Vanished City* from Time-Life Books).[3]

Procedure

1. The lesson begins with a discrepant event inquiry.[4] The inquiry is followed by discussion and finally a K-W-L. Developed by Donna Ogle, K-W-L is an acronym for the process that students go through during the course of a learning experience. The "K" stands for "what I Know," and is discussed and recorded early in the lesson in order to get at prior knowledge; "W" is "what I Want to know," and involves discussing/listing questions of interest to students prior to the learning experience; and "L" is "what I Learned," and is completed at the closure point in the lesson.[5]

This is the inquiry I have developed to begin the lesson on Pompeii:

You and a friend are walking through a quaint old city. The summer sun warms the rooftops of the old homes. Listening to birds singing and the curious voices of small children and their parents, you notice a mansion a block or so to your left. Walking over to the large home, you see an outdoor patio with a table set for dinner. Next to the patio is a doghouse. A woman outside mopping the patio looks up and smiles at you.

As you enter the business district, you remark to your friend how small the stores are and how close they are to one another. While you are talking, you notice a bakery to your left. An oven door is open, and you see several loaves of bread ready to be taken out. Just then, a small girl and her father pass in front of you. The girl looks up to her father and asks why nobody is at home or at work. The father looks down at her, smiles, and says, "Well, no one lives in this city."

The problem that students must figure out is stated thus: "You have traveled through this city, seen some of its homes and businesses with evidence of life all around you, and yet no one lives in it. How is this possible?"

After the problem statement is given, students begin to question the teacher in an attempt to figure out the puzzle, but they can only ask questions that can be answered with a "yes" or a "no". For instance, they might begin by asking, "Is the city actually a Hollywood set?" (the answer would be "no") or "Is this a real city?" (the answer would be "yes"). Questions build upon questions, and answers become further questions as the inquiry moves along. Stop the students from time to time to have them discuss and hypothesize in their small groups. From this point, it is not difficult for them to realize that the characters in the short story were walking through a city that was abandoned or destroyed. One possible answer to this inquiry, and the one that I bring up, is that "your friend, yourself, and the other people are tourists and the city is Pompeii—an uninhabited city in Italy that was destroyed by the volcano Vesuvius almost two thousand years ago."

Following the completion of the inquiry, we discuss the process of discovering what happened in Pompeii. At this point we begin recording in notebooks what we are beginning to learn about Pompeii. The format that I often use as we are going through the interactive presentation is the previously mentioned K-W-L. We begin with the "K" as students begin listing what they know, or think they know, about Pompeii. While students are in groups, they are asked to make a group list using a structure known as cooperative structure "roundtable." In roundtable, a sheet of paper is passed around the group as members discuss and make note of what they believe they know about Pompeii.[6] We discuss their prior knowledge.

We have done the inquiry and discussed/written on students' prior knowledge and what they would like to learn. We move to the second part, which is to have a quick presentation focusing on developing interest and further questions regarding the subject matter.

2. The second part of the interactive presentation is a short media presentation/mini-lecture on the topic. The purpose is to have the students view a short segment of a video that presents some information on the topic (in this case Pompeii), or perhaps a slide that is augmented with some verbal information. This presents students with a visual cue that whets their appetite to see and learn more about the subject.

After reviewing a number of different media presentations on Pompeii, I have selected a segment of the Time-Life video program *Rome: The Ultimate Empire* (from the "Lost Civilizations" series).[7] The segment that I show students lasts about five minutes and is the section on Pompeii.

This video segment begins with narration, "One ancient city in Southern Italy epitomized the commerce, prosperity, and vitality enjoyed at the heart of empire. [The video shows people in tunics walking in a dimly lit street at night.] Its streets were alive into the night. Twenty thousand Romans lived here." The video segment goes on to show a family beginning to eat dinner when Vesuvius explodes. Following a moving reenactment of a Pompeian family caught in the explosion, this segment of the video then goes on to show ancient frescos from Pompeii and ruins of the city, and the narrator explains that through the efforts of archaeologists, life in Pompeii is being revealed. The video goes on to show old pictures of an archaeological dig and explains, "In 1860, Giuseppe Fiorelli made the first systematic excavation of Pompeii. On a hunch, Fiorelli poured plaster into cavities he suspected were made by human remains. From the earthen molds the victims emerged." The video continues with scenes of the plaster casts of the dead on a street in Pompeii with a sad violin accompaniment. As the camera pans up a hardened ash hill, we hear, "This gang of ancient construction workers struggled to stay on top only to be struck down by a shockwave of volcanic gas." At this point, I stop the video and we work through the "W" section of the K-W-L, as we discuss and list questions students would like to know about Pompeii.

From this introduction, we move to the next section of the interactive presentation: the cooperative discussion group. Prior to this activity, two quotes from the video are mentioned to students: "Ironically, Vesuvius preserved as well as destroyed Pompeii," and "a surprising mosaic of life is revealed." Students are told to keep the two statements in mind as they look at the accounts of Pompeii by an archaeologist, an eyewitness, and a geologist.

3. The third part of the interactive presentation is the use of cooperative learning.[8] In the group work, students examine evidence from primary and secondary sources that help them form their own answers to these questions.

Each group is given a folder with three information sheets (see appendix). The first information sheet contains a geological account of the explosion, the second, a discussion of an archaeological perspective on Pompeii, and the third, quotations from the letters of Pliny the Younger, an eyewitness to the explosion (this primary source represents the historical view). The information sheets also contain questions that ask students to think about and discuss what they have. Each information sheet also contains a picture that relates to the content. They also contain enough information that, through synthesis, students could put together to get a clear picture of what life was like in Pompeii, the explosion, and how that explosion destroyed and yet preserved Pompeii.

The cooperative groups of three begin by dividing the information sheets among the group members. Each student takes the information sheet that he or she received, scans it, and then passes it to his or her left. This is done quickly until each student has seen each information sheet. Students are then given directions so that they can carefully go over one information sheet at a time, read it, and discuss the questions together. After they have developed their ideas about the reading and the discussion questions, students put the ideas in their notebooks (and thus begin to work on the "L" part of the K-W-L—what they are learning). Using the "task-group share group" strategy,[9] students share their ideas with other groups. In this strategy, one student from each group will rotate between all other groups every few minutes. We begin by having one group member move to the group on the right, discuss what his or her previous group thought, and then he or she moves onto the next group. When this activity is complete, all students will be back in their original group with ideas from every other group in the room. This activity is followed by a classroom discussion that deals with the historical, archaeological, and geological perspectives on Pompeii.

4. The fourth phase of the interactive presentation is a writing for understanding activity.[10] This is an individual assignment in which students write creatively about the uncovering of Pompeii. In this lesson, students are given a number of different possibilities for their writing assignment. They may, for example, write a historian's guide to Pompeii for visitors or assume the role of a student archaeologist and write an article for the local paper.

5. The fifth and final phase of the interactive presentation is the whole class discussion/review. Based on ideas contained with the Teachers' Curriculum Institute's *History Alive!*[11] and the Interactive Slide Lecture,[12] and using a number of Merrill Harmin's Inspiring Active Learning techniques,[13] this final section seeks to synthesize the ideas of this lesson via discussion and writing.

Media images are used to illustrate and elicit discussion over the main ideas presented in the lesson. In this case, I once again use the Time-Life video *Rome: The Ultimate Empire.*[14] As with the phase just prior to the cooperative activity, the section of that video on Pompeii is used. It lasts only five minutes, and with the knowledge and understanding that students have gained, the segment becomes more meaningful, more moving, and a prompt for further discussion.

The discussion is centered on the two statements that students were told to watch for: that Vesuvius both destroyed and preserved Pompeii, and that a surprising mosaic of life was revealed by archaeologists. As further prompts to discussion, several slides are used. The first shows an artist's conception of Roman citizens in the market place, and the second shows the volcanic eruption and people fleeing. The third shows some of the human plaster of Paris molds. When each slide is shown to students, they are asked to do a "sharing pairs" [15] in order to discuss what is happening in the slide. Students then discuss and, at times, role play the people in the slides.[16] For example, volunteer students will stand in front of the slide of people walking through the streets of Pompeii and answer questions, from other students and myself, as if they were those people in the slide. When the slide is projected showing the human casts, several students will go up to the slide and assume the role of archaeologists. Questions will be asked about the uncovering of Pompeii and these bodies. Discussion revolves around the slide images and the student reactions to them.

We complete the lesson with students taking notes by responding in writing to several prompts given to them in class.[17] The prompts would include finishing the following sentence stems: "I learned that . . ." and "I still wonder . . .". The writing serves both as notes in students' notebooks and a summary of their learning completing the K-W-L cycle.

Assessment
Students write an essay that can be based on a variety of roles or possibilities. There are a number of criteria that the essay must contain regardless of the role they assume. It must contain students' ideas of (1) what Pompeii was like prior to the explosion, (2) the explosion and its effects, and (3) the archaeological evidence left behind. Student opportunities to develop their ideas come primarily from the cooperative learning activity and would necessitate synthesizing the geological, archaeological, and eye-witness discussions.

Prior to beginning their first drafts, students are presented with an assessment rubric (see appendix). The rubric is discussed in class. After working through a couple of drafts, and reading in pairs, students move to the computer lab to create the final version of their essay. In addition to their writing, students are to incorporate sketches, diagrams, maps, and/or other visuals. This writing assignment is coordinated with the language arts teacher. Thus, the writing that students do in social studies must meet criteria that they have in language arts (e.g., spelling, topic sentences, structure).

Conclusion
In the four days of learning and thinking about Pompeii, students are involved in an in-depth examination of the life, death, and resurrection of Pompeii using the processes of inquiry, cooperative learning, and writing for understanding. In doing so, students analyze and synthesize information from a geologic perspective, an archaeological perspective, and a historical perspective (an eyewitness account). The format of the lesson, the interactive presentation, and the materials used attempt to help students build on the process of inquiry, socially construct their own understanding of Pompeii, and develop a creative essay demonstrating their new understanding.

Nearly two thousand years ago, a tragedy of cataclysmic proportions occurred in Pompeii. In attempting to understand the humanity and dimensions of that tragedy, students can come to a deeper and more personal understanding of life in the ancient world. ▨

Notes

1. Michael M. Yell, "The Time Before History: Thinking Like an Archaeologist," *Social Education* 62, no. 1 (1998): 27-31.

2. "Lost Civilizations," *Rome: The Ultimate Empire*, video (Alexandria, Va.: Time-Life Video and Television, 1995).

3. "Lost Civilizations," *Pompeii: The Vanished City*, video (Alexandria, Va.: Time-Life Books, 1992).

4. B. Joyce, M. Weil, and B. Showers, *Models of Teaching* (Needham Heights, Mass.: Allyn and Bacon, 1994); W. Bruce and J. Bruce, *Teaching Social Studies with Discrepant Event Inquiry* (Annapolis, Md.: Alpha Publishing Co., 1992).

5. K-W-L is discussed in many sources including R. Marzano, D. Pickering, R. Brandt, et al., *Teacher's Manual: Dimensions of Learning* (Alexandria, Va.: Association for Supervision and Curriculum Development, 1992); and Merrill Harmin, *Strategies to Inspire Active Learning* (Edwardsville, Ill.: Inspiring Strategies Institute, 1996).

6. S. Kagan, *Cooperative Learning* (San Clemente, Calif.: Kagan Cooperative Learning, 1995).

7. "Lost Civilizations," Rome, 1995. I have found that it is best to use videotapes in small segments with opportunities for interaction rather than showing them in their entirety. For example, I use a great deal of the video *Rome: The Ultimate Empire*, but I spread the video out through several lessons.

8. Kagan, *Cooperative Learning*, 1995; B. Bower, J. Lobdell, and L. Swenson, *History Alive! Engaging All Learners in the Diverse Classroom* (New York: Addison-Wesley, 1994).

9. Harmin, *Strategies to Inspire Active Learning*, 1996.

10. Bower, Lobdell, and Swenson, *History Alive!*, 1994.

11. *Ibid.*

12. *Ibid.*

13. Harmin, *Strategies to Inspire Active Learning*, 1996.

14. "Lost Civilizations," Rome, 1995.

15. Harmin, *Strategies to Inspire Active Learning*, 1996.

16. See the Interactive Slide Lecture discussion in Bower, Lobdell, and Swenson, 1995, for a further explanation of role playing to the images in slides.

17. See discussion of Outcome Statements in Harmin, *Strategies to Inspire Active Learning*, 1996.

THE GEOLOGICAL VIEW

In 79 AD, Pompeii was destroyed and, ironically, preserved by the massive explosion of the volcano Vesuvius. For several years before that explosion, there had been signals from Mt. Vesuvius that today we would know indicate a possible eruption. In 62 AD, a great earthquake destroyed many buildings in Pompeii. The earthquake was the result of magma pressure (magma is rock melted by the rubbing together of tectonic plates—the giant slabs of rock that the crust of the earth is divided into). Having no idea that the earthquake was a signal of future danger, the people went about rebuilding their city.

By the year 79 AD, there were other disturbing signs. Wells and springs were drying up. This was caused by the heat of the magma turning the ground water to steam. In early August, a series of small earthquakes was felt throughout Pompeii as pressure built. In the early morning of August 24, a series of steam explosions burst through the floor of the crater at the top of Mt. Vesuvius. The crater is a plug of hardened lava that seals the "throat" of a volcano.

Then in the early afternoon, a tremendous blast blew off the top of the mountain. Vesuvius became a giant cannon with its muzzle turned up toward the sky. Tons of molten rock shot roughly fifteen miles into the sky at perhaps twice the speed of sound. The ash and small rock particles blew upward, eventually losing momentum and flattening out into a great black cloud. The winds were blowing in the direction of Pompeii.

By mid-afternoon a cloud of ash had made the day as dark as night. From this black sky came a downpour of rocks and ash. The seemingly endless snow of ash and stones fell at the rate of about six inches every hour. By midnight, the ash was over six feet deep (by the time the explosion was over, Pompeii was buried in about twenty feet of ash). Those who had not been crushed to death, suffocated, or died of heart attacks, went into the streets. They did not know that the worst was yet to come.

Early in the morning of the 25th, a surge, sometimes called a death cloud, raced down the mountain. A volcanic surge is a fast moving, ground hugging, cloud of ash, rock particles, and poisonous gas. The death cloud may have been moving at a rate of over one hundred miles per hour and may have reached temperatures as high as 750° Fahrenheit. The death cloud blew apart and incinerated anything in its path.

Discussion

1. From the geologist's description, explain what happened to the people and the city of Pompeii as if you were an eyewitness.
2. It is said that this explosion both destroyed and preserved Pompeii. How could it do both?
3. Discuss your list of what you want to know ("W"). How does this reading answer any of your questions?

THE ARCHAEOLOGICAL VIEW

For years after Pompeii had become an ash-covered graveyard, there were stories of a lost city by Vesuvius. In the year 1594, a wealthy count wanted to have water from the river Sarno on his property, which lies just south of Vesuvius. The workmen dug through the volcanic rock and uncovered the ruins of an ancient building with the words "decurion Pompeiss". Soon it was forgotten. In 1748, Spanish engineers discovered the ruins of an ancient temple and a skeleton with bronze and silver coins scattered beside it. The Spanish engineers apparently had little interest in unearthing the lost city. Their main interest seemed to be finding money and trophies. A hunt for treasure in the lost city began. The identity of the city became known when the workers came upon an inscription that read "res publica Pompeianorum."

The diggers moved from area to area, making shafts and tunnels, and finding and taking what might be valuable. The looting and search for treasure continued on, inflicting a great deal of damage on the ruins of Pompeii. However, the interests of scholars who were more interested in investigating the past and preserving the lost city than looting began to take hold. In 1860, the king of Italy, who understood the importance of Pompeii to his country's history, hired a group of workers to carefully uncover and examine Pompeii. His most important contribution was appointing the head of the excavation, Giuseppe Fiorelli.

Giuseppe Fiorelli led the first systematic archaeological dig of Pompeii. He carefully quarried through the volcanic rock, found a wall that surrounded much of the city, and divided the site into sections called regiones. He made certain every new find was precisely described in writing in terms of its appearance, its position, and its relationship to other objects. During his work one day, Giuseppe began thinking about how the ash had covered everything and become hardened. He reasoned that cavities that had been found in the rock had been made by human bodies covered by the hardened ash. Acting on this belief, when cavities would be found, he had them filled with liquid plaster of Paris. When the rock was chipped away, plaster molds of the victims of Vesuvius emerged. The people were in the exact position of their death.

Over the years, archaeological finds have revealed much about life in Pompeii. Some finds include the following:

- A mansion on the outskirts of town with farm implements in the main room, some even hung on walls over paintings;
- Graffiti all over the city including a statement that reads, "Successus the cloth-weaver loves Iris, the innkeeper's slave girl";
- A large outdoor arena with the bodies of fifty men found nearby; some in chains;
- Large mansions, some with over fifty rooms, and along the streets, dozens of smaller buildings with even smaller attached buildings opening into the streets;
- Rooms with food, long dried out, but often still on the dinner table or in the oven, as well as household effects, from jewelry to cosmetics to perfume;
- In the western end of the city, a large rectangular area (500 feet long by 150 feet) without buildings but surrounded by statues and large columns; and
- A large wall found on one end of this huge rectangular area containing over a thousand painted phrases. One such phrase was "Support Sabinus and he will support you."

Discussion
1. Explain how archaeologists have uncovered Pompeii.
2. Choose at least four of the examples of the archaeological findings discussed and explain what they tell us about what life in Pompeii was like.
3. Explain how the finds of archaeologists support what geologists say about the explosion of Vesuvius.
4. Discuss your list of what you want to know ("W"). How does this reading answer any of your questions?

THE HISTORICAL VIEW (An Eyewitness Account)

Almost twenty miles from Pompeii, at the naval base of Misenum, seventeen-year-old Pliny the Younger watched the explosion. Although he experienced many of the same effects of Vesuvius, because of the distance involved, those effects were not as deadly. The following are from his eyewitness account of the explosion:

"The cloud was rising. . . . In appearance and shape it was like a tree. Like an immense pine tree for it shot up to a great height in the form of a tree trunk, which extended itself at the top into several branches. It was dark and spotted, as if it had carried up earth and cinders. My uncle [Pliny the Elder] deemed the phenomenon important and worth a nearer view."

"Though it was the first hour of the afternoon, the light was faint and uncertain. The buildings around us were so unsettled that the collapse of walls seemed a certainty. We decided to get out of town to escape this menace. The panic-stricken crowds followed us, in response to that instinct of fear which causes people to follow where others lead."

"When we were clear of the houses we stopped. The sea appeared to have shrunk as if they had withdrawn by tremors of the earth. Many sea creatures were dead on the shore. Behind us loomed a horrible black cloud ripped by sudden bursts of fire, writhing snakelike and revealing sudden flashes larger than lightning. We ran."

"Soon afterward the cloud began to descend upon the earth and cover the sea. Ashes fell upon us. Though as yet of no great quantity, I looked behind me. Darkness came rolling over the land like a torrent. I proposed, while we could still see, [to stop and rest]. We had just sat down when darkness overspread us, not like that of a moonless or cloudy night, but of a room when it is shut up and the lamp put out. You could hear the shrieks of women and crying children and the shouts of men; some were seeking their children, others their parents; some praying to die, from the very fear of dying; many lifting their hands to the gods, but the greater part imagining that there were no gods left anywhere. That the last and eternal night was come upon the world."

Discussion

1. Describe what it might have been like to be in Pompeii during the explosion of Vesuvius.
2. Explain how Pliny's account compares to the geologist's and archaeologist's accounts.
3. Discuss your list of what you want to know ("W"). How does this reading answer any of your questions?

Rubric for Pompeii Essay

5. Highly Proficient

- Essay presents the three criteria in a factual and creative manner.
- Essay develops student's ideas about Pompeii and explores them in depth.
- Essay has correct format including illustrations, topic sentences, spelling, and grammar.

4. Proficient

- The essay presents the three assignment criteria in a factual manner.
- Essay elaborates on student ideas about Pompeii.
- Essay shows generally good format including illustrations, grammar, and spelling.

3. Partially Proficient

- The essay contains several of the assignment criteria in a factual manner.
- The essay discusses student ideas about Pompeii.
- Essay contains illustrations but has several grammatical errors.

2. Minimally Proficient

- The essay contains several of the assignment criteria.
- Elaboration of student ideas about Pompeii is lacking.
- Essay contains many grammatical and structural errors.

0. Unacceptable/Redo

- Essay does not contain assignment criteria.
- Essay does not elaborate on ideas.
- Essay contains many grammatical and structural errors.

Global Reflections in Economic Decision Making

Suzanne C. Zaremba, J. B. Fisher Model Elementary, Richmond Public Schools, Richmond, Virginia

Grade Level/Subject: Third Grade—Social Studies

NCSS Thematic Strands:

⑦ PRODUCTION, DISTRIBUTION, AND CONSUMPTION (Early Grades)

a. give examples that show how scarcity and choice govern our economic decisions;

b. distinguish between wants and needs;

g. explain and demonstrate the role of money in everyday life; and

i. use economic concepts such as supply, demand, and price to help explain events in the community and nation.

⑨ GLOBAL CONNECTIONS (Early Grades)

b. give examples of conflict, cooperation, and interdependence among individuals, groups, and nations; and

e. examine the relationships and tensions between personal wants and needs and various global concerns, such as the use of imported oil, land use, and environmental protection.

Key Features of Powerful Teaching and Learning

Meaningful—to many students in the intermediate grades, economics has little meaning because Mom and Dad usually hand out the money for wants or pay for the necessities. This lesson will become meaningful as the students learn, through an in-depth inquiry project, the difference between wants and needs, supply and demand, scarcity and choice, and the interdependence between people individually and globally. In the long run, hopefully, students will learn how economic decision making will directly and indirectly affect their lives;

Integrative—this lesson integrates knowledge, skills, and attitudes to action. Students will apply math skills to understand the financial decisions in designing and building such a project. Good communication skills will be needed to help pave the way to negotiate for needed goods. Critical thinking skills must be applied as the groups must find ways to achieve their goals. A knowledge of culture and living styles will add immensely to the artistic and practical decisions in style and function;

Value-based—in the negotiating process, the students will deal with the problems of conflict, cooperation, and interdependence among individuals, groups, and nations. They will have to examine the relationships between wants and needs and various global concerns. They will have to make value judgments regarding the priorities of these concerns and relationships;

Challenging—students must be creative designers, negotiators, and builders to solve an inquiry problem. Negotiating will offer a challenge in that each group will see the reasoning of working together to achieve its goals. The students will learn that interdependence between individuals and nations develops through knowledge of the responsibilities needed to complete certain exchanges based on supply and demand; and

Active—students are actively constructing knowledge as they interact, make decisions, and solve an authentic real-life problem. This is a "hands on" activity to help promote the realization of the need to work cooperatively in our world economy. The students will learn that in many situations, supply and demand and scarcity and choice determine the relationships between countries. The student groups will experience the negotiating process directly through the planned activity. The groups should realize that they must reassess their decisions throughout the negotiation process in order to complete their task successfully.

Purpose/Rationale/Introduction

Japan is a small island country with limited space and limited natural resources. Because of these limitations, the Japanese greatly depend on the imported resources of other countries. Through this lesson, students will identify and interpret economic principles. Students will learn to understand that scarcity is universal and is not eliminated by the wealth of an individual or a nation. Students will learn how scarcity and choice govern economic needs. Students will also learn to distinguish between wants and needs and to experience decision-making skills based on the theory of supply and demand.

This lesson plan is from a unit developed on "Today's Japan." Prior to this lesson, the class will have studied many facets of modern Japan including viewing a video of Japanese life and culture. This video will be shown at the beginning of the unit to help students develop an understanding of the simplicity and efficiency of the Japanese way of using available space and materials. Also, before using this lesson, the class will be introduced to the concepts of international trade and economic interdependence through other units like "The Development of Virginia" and through issues in the newspaper during weekly current events sessions.

Objectives (Students will):

a. recognize the usable amount of land mass in Japan;

b. compare and contrast land mass and population versus scarcity and choice;

c. compare wants and needs in Japanese culture and society with wants and needs in their own society;

d. summarize the principle that limited resources (scarcity) versus relatively unlimited wants (uses) for the resources is a central economic problem that requires choices to be made by individuals or nations;

e. describe how the theory of supply and demand can determine our economic decisions;

f. explain how basic human needs are universal;

g. discover how limited natural resources can affect tensions and relationships in the global economy;

h. experience the importance of decision making and the impact of consequences;

i.   research and make a list of the land mass problems of Japan;

j.   research and define "limited natural resources" in Japan;

k.   implement effective trading strategies by working in cooperative groups to negotiate; and

l.   demonstrate through cooperative learning groups the complexities and issues pertaining to interdependence and international trade.

Time Allotment—two class sessions of forty-five minutes to one hour and one class session of one and one-half hours (three sessions in all)

Resources Needed

1. six large bags or boxes with a variation of the following supplies:

   paper
   scissors
   tag board
   rubber bands
   wooden popsicle sticks
   rice paper
   string
   pen or pencil
   glue
   ruler
   tape
   cardboard shingles
   straw mat pieces
   tacks
   paper clips
   eraser
   small stones
   crayons or markers or colored pencils
   mat board pieces
   exacto knife or mat knife (assorted sizes)
   child's hammer
   tiny nails
   play money
   sheet of foam board
   thin tracing paper
   child's saw
   pictures of possible trade items

2. a task card for each cooperative group (see appendix);

3. a discussion sheet for each cooperative group (see appendix);

4. a classroom resource center with books about Japanese culture, housing, geography, and economy (including a world atlas and a world almanac); and

5. a common list of economic terms and their definitions (see appendix).

Procedure

First Session—Directions for Task (approximately one hour)

1. The students will have prior knowledge pertaining to this task from other lessons in the unit. For the first fifteen minutes of this period, the teacher will divide the class into six groups, explaining that each group will represent a building contractor from a country that is about to build a Japanese style house. The teacher will assign each group the name of the country it is to represent.

2. The teacher will have each group (or country) designate a leader, a trade representative (negotiator), a recorder or bookkeeper, a researcher, and two laborers.

3. Each group will be given a large bag or box with supplies that represents that country's readily available building products, possible trade resources, task cards, a house plan, and discussion sheets. No country will have the same materials. Some of the countries will have more than others, some almost nothing; others will be well supplied. Each group will receive a bag or box of supplies according to the resources associated with its country.

First Session—Group Organization

1. Within the next fifteen-minute period, have the group work with and understand each person's designated job as it applies to the task.

2. Within this same time constraint, have the six groups look at their allocated supplies. The recorder/bookkeeper will record the reactions of the group members during the distribution of supplies. Each country will need to trade its resources or products in the world market (six countries) to get the products to complete its task.

3. During the rest of this session, each group should review its task card, determine its situation, make decisions, and make plans for completing the task assigned.

Second Session—Negotiating/Building Time (approximately one and one-half hours)

This session will give each group ample time to first review the task and jobs. From there, it will take the remaining time for the cooperative group to proceed with the purpose of the task assignment. It will take time, work, and creative thinking to acquire the needed materials to build. Working smart as a team will help produce the end product. Some groups may not have a complete product due to many different factors as the process evolves. Interdependence and cooperation is not always an easy process.

Third Session—forty-five minutes (approximately one hour)

Upon completion of the task, the groups will reconvene as a class. After each group has made a five-minute presentation on its products, group members will then participate in a discussion based on the following questions (the discussion sheet should have been given out previously with the supply package. This would provide thought for the discussion period):

a. How did you feel when you saw the disparities in resources from one country to the other?

b. How does scarcity necessitate decision making?

c. What were some of the problems encountered in the trading process?

d. How does this activity reflect the real-world situation?

e. Does trading help or hinder other countries and their economies? Why and how?

f. How do the resources of Japan and its economy determine its role in the building industry of that particular country?

Assessment

Group assessment will be measured by the completed task and the effective or ineffective trading strategies implemented to complete the task. The group will make presentations of its project and explain the strategies used.

Individual assessment will be twofold. First, each group must evaluate the participation of each of its members using the categories of fair, good, and excellent. Second, each member of the class must list in writing ways that Japan's economic system is connected to or dependent on other countries.

Extension and Enrichment

Plan and design a Japanese garden in an allotted space outside the classroom. Use productive thinking skills and newly acquired economic decision-making skills to find or acquire the needed materials to make the garden a reality. This garden should be a symbol that reflects the essence of beauty and nature in the Japanese culture. It can be your gift to the enhancement of your school grounds for all to enjoy.

Using a map of Japan, take a one-inch square, and let it represent Tokyo. Place the square in another area of Japan. Explain your reasoning for wanting to locate that city in another area and the economic implications that might go with such a move.

Teacher Resource List

Videos

Japan: The Island—Empire. San Ramon, CA: International Video Network, 1984.

Kansai, Japan's Gateway to the Next Century (possible to borrow from a Japan America Society).

Books

The Cambridge Encyclopedia of Japan Cambridge: Cambridge University Press, 1993.

Christopher, Robert C. *The Japanese Mind.* United Kingdom: Pan Books, 1984.

Exploring Your World. Washington, D.C.: National Geographic Society, 1989.

The Japan of Today. Tokyo, Japan: The International Society for Educational Information, Inc., 1993.

Langone, John. *In the Shogun's Shadow: Understanding a Changing Japan.* Canada: Little, Brown, and Co., 1994.

A Look into Japan. Tokyo, Japan: Japan Travel Bureau, Inc., 1994.

Today's Japan. Tokyo, Japan: Japan Travel Bureau, Inc., 1994.

Views of Japan. Tokyo, Japan: Urban Connections, Inc., 1995.

Wojtan, Linda. *Resources for Teaching about Japan.* Bloomington, Ind.: ERIC Clearinghouse for Social Studies/Social Science Education, The National Clearinghouse for United States—Japan Studies, 1993.

Yagi, Kaji. *A Japanese Touch for Your Home.* New York: Kodanska International, 1992.

TASK CARD

The purpose of this assignment is to teach you that interdependence between individuals as well as nations plays a role in our economic system. What is that role? You will find the answers to that as you proceed with the task.

You have been assigned to a group that represents a certain country. Each person in your group will have a job to do during this project. Working cooperatively as a group in your individual jobs will help to move your group along smoothly and help to accomplish the task you have been given.

Your task is to build a Japanese style house with the materials needed to complete the job. Your country may be rich or poor in resources according to what you will find in the bag or box of supplies. If you need supplies different from those you have been given, you must become resourceful. Decision making, planning, and negotiating are all part of the process. Who has what you need? Do you have something another country can use? What kind of deals and how many might you have to make to get your house built? Record each trade or transaction. Build your house.

Job Descriptions

Leader
- guides the group by setting a good example
- helps all members participate
- keeps the group focused on the job

As Leader I Will:
- read clearly so that everyone in my group can hear.
- share the group's ideas with the class.
- keep the group working on the job.

Recorder/Bookkeeper
- listens closely to each member
- writes down important information
- keeps a tally of materials traded

As Recorder I Will:
- write or draw the group's ideas.
- be a good listener.
- keep a record of materials traded.

Researcher
- finds needed information
- makes sure the members are informed
- encourages the group

As a Researcher I Will:
- look up all the information as it is needed.
- give all members useful information.
- support others by helping.

Trade Representative
- gets needed materials for the group
- delivers materials and messages
- puts materials away

As a Trade Representative I Will:
- negotiate for needed materials to complete our task.
- go for help when needed.
- take care of the building materials.

Two Laborers
- notify the group of the starting and stopping times
- keep track of the remaining time and encourage the group to continue
- keep the group working on the job

As a Laborer I Will:
- start the building on time.
- help keep the group on task.
- help others to do their best.

Discussion Sheet

Group _____

Date _____

Group Peer Evaluation:

Effective	Ineffective	Comments

a.   How did you feel when you saw the disparities in resources from one country to the other?

b.   How does scarcity necessitate decision making?

c.   What were some of the problems encountered in the trading process?

d.   How does this activity reflect the real-world situation?

e.   Does trading help or hinder other countries and their economies? Why and how?

f.   How do the resources of Japan and its economy determine its role in the building industry of that particular country?

Floor Plan for Japanese Home

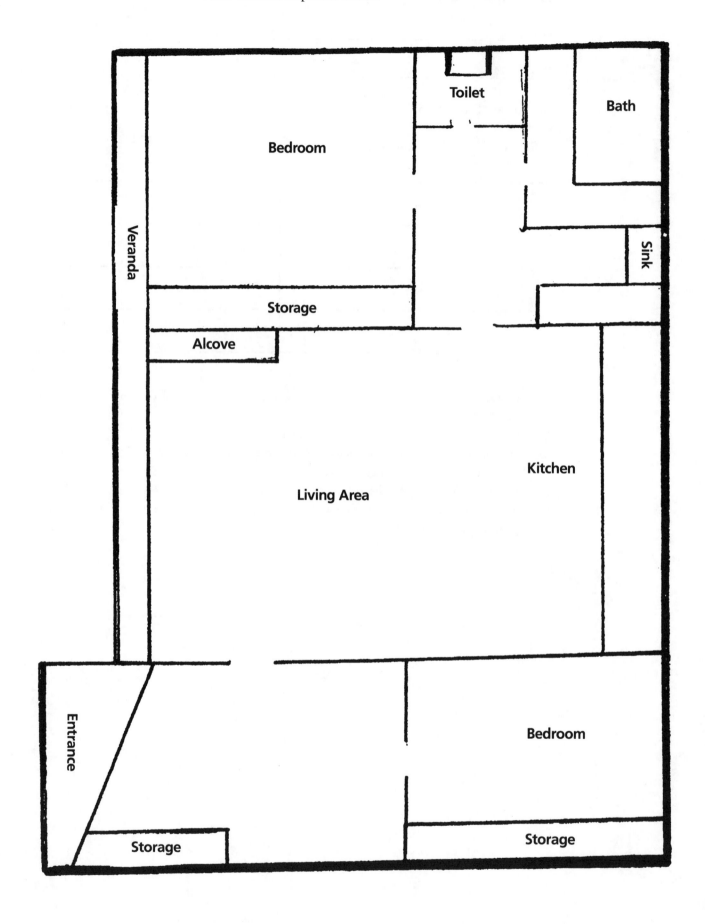

COMMON ECONOMIC TERMS AND DEFINITIONS

- Barter—the direct exchange of goods and services.

- Business (firm)—a privately owned, profit-oriented organization engaged in the buying and hiring of resources, and in the production and sale of goods and services.

- Choice making (wants-income gap)—a result of scarcity. Because we have unlimited wants for goods and services and have only limited income, we must choose what goods and services will be produced.

- Consumer—person who uses goods and services to satisfy wants directly.

- Consumer goods—tangible objects that are scarce and satisfy consumer wants.

- Consumer services—productive acts that satisfy consumer wants, but do not result in tangible objects.

- Division of labor—the separation of production into various tasks performed by different workers, allowing specialization and the development and use of higher and more productive human skills.

- Efficiency—producing a maximum amount of goods and services with a given amount of resources or producing a given amount of goods and services with a minimum amount of resources.

- Government income—the total of money payments received by government, generally in the form of taxes.

- Marketplace—occurs whenever individuals are engaged in the process of buying and selling goods and services.

- Medium of exchange—one of the functions of money whereby people exchange goods and services for money and in turn use money to obtain other goods and services.

- Money—anything that is generally acceptable in exchange (payment) for goods and services. Credit cards take the place of money, but they are not direct payments for goods or services.

- Money income (earned)—money payments during a given time period received for performance of a productive act.